P9-CMF-641

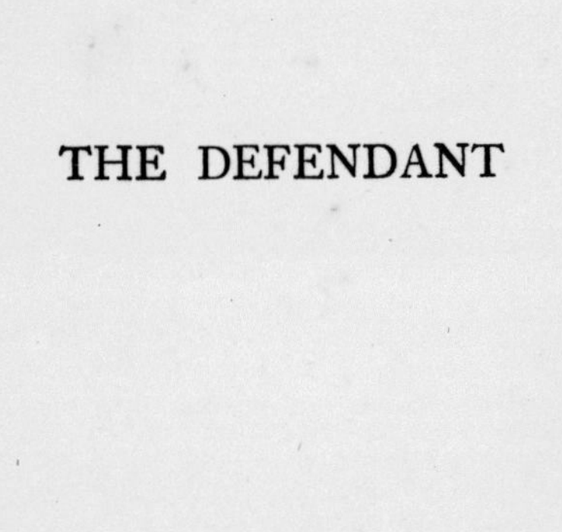

THE DEFENDANT

THE DEFENDANT

BY G. K. CHESTERTON

AUTHOR OF 'THE WILD KNIGHT'
AND 'GREYBEARDS AT PLAY'

LONDON. MDCCCCI
R. BRIMLEY JOHNSON

The 'Defences' of which this volume is composed have appeared in *The Speaker*, and are here reprinted, after revision and amplification, by permission of the Editor. Portions of 'The Defence of Publicity' appeared in *The Daily News*.

October, 1901.

CONTENTS

THE DEFENDANT

INTRODUCTION

IN certain endless uplands, uplands like great flats gone dizzy, slopes that seem to contradict the idea that there is even such a thing as a level, and make us all realize that we live on a planet with a sloping roof, you will come from time to time upon whole valleys filled with loose rocks and boulders, so big as to be like mountains broken loose. The whole might be an experimental creation shattered and cast away. It is often difficult to believe that such cosmic refuse can have come together except by human means. The mildest and most cockney imagination conceives the place to be the scene of some war of giants. To me it is always associated with one idea, recurrent and at last instinctive. The scene was the scene of the stoning of some prehistoric prophet, a prophet as much more gigantic than after-prophets as the boulders are more gigantic than the pebbles. He spoke some words—words that seemed shameful and tremendous—and the world, in terror, buried him under a wilderness of stones. The place is the monument of an ancient fear.

If we followed the same mood of fancy, it would be more difficult to imagine what awful hint or wild picture of the universe called forth that primal persecution, what secret of sensational thought lies buried under the brutal stones. For in our time the blasphemies are threadbare. Pessimism is now patently, as it always was essentially, more commonplace than piety. Profanity is now more than an affectation—it is a convention. The curse against God is Exercise I. in the primer of minor poetry. It was not, assuredly, for such babyish solemnities that our imaginary prophet was stoned in the morning of the world. If we weigh the matter in the faultless scales of imagination, if we see what is the real trend of humanity, we shall feel it most probable that he was stoned for saying that the grass was green and that the birds sang in spring; for the mission of all the prophets from the beginning has not been so much the pointing out of heavens or hells as primarily the pointing out of the earth.

Religion has had to provide that longest and strangest telescope — the telescope through which we could see the star upon which we dwelt. For the mind and eyes of the average man this world is as lost as Eden and as sunken as Atlantis. There runs a strange law through the length of human history—that men are continually tending to undervalue their environment, to undervalue their happiness, to undervalue themselves. The great sin of mankind, the sin typified by the fall of Adam, is the tendency, not towards pride, but towards this weird and horrible humility.

This is the great fall, the fall by which the fish forgets the sea, the ox forgets the meadow, the clerk forgets the city, every man forgets his environment and, in the fullest and most literal sense, forgets himself. This is the real fall of Adam, and it is a spiritual fall. It is a strange thing that many truly spiritual men, such as General Gordon, have actually spent some hours in speculating upon the precise location of the Garden of Eden. Most probably we are in Eden still. It is only our eyes that have changed.

The pessimist is commonly spoken of as

the man in revolt. He is not. Firstly, because it requires some cheerfulness to continue in revolt, and secondly, because pessimism appeals to the weaker side of everybody, and the pessimist, therefore, drives as roaring a trade as the publican. The person who is really in revolt is the optimist, who generally lives and dies in a desperate and suicidal effort to persuade all the other people how good they are. It has been proved a hundred times over that if you really wish to enrage people and make them angry, even unto death, the right way to do it is to tell them that they are all the sons of God. Jesus Christ was crucified, it may be remembered, not because of anything he said about God, but on a charge of saying that a man could in three days pull down and rebuild the Temple. Every one of the great revolutionists, from Isaiah to Shelley, have been optimists. They have been indignant, not about the badness of existence, but about the slowness of men in realizing its goodness. The prophet who is stoned is not a brawler or a marplot. He is simply a rejected lover. He suffers from an unrequited attachment to things in general.

It becomes increasingly apparent, therefore, that the world is in a permanent danger of being misjudged. That this is no fanciful or mystical idea may be tested by simple examples. The two absolutely basic words ‘good’ and ‘bad,’ descriptive of two primal and inexplicable sensations, are not, and never have been, used properly. Things that are bad are not called good by any people who experience them; but things that are good are called bad by the universal verdict of humanity.

Let me explain a little: Certain things are bad so far as they go, such as pain, and no one, not even a lunatic, calls a toothache good in itself; but a knife which cuts clumsily and with difficulty is called a bad knife, which it certainly is not. It is only not so good as other knives to which men have grown accustomed. A knife is never bad except on such rare occasions as that in which it is neatly and scientifically planted in the middle of one's back. The coarsest and bluntest knife which ever broke a pencil into pieces instead of sharpening it is a good thing in so far as it is a knife. It would have appeared a miracle in the Stone Age. What we call a bad knife is a good knife not good enough for us; what we call a bad hat is a good hat not good enough for us; what we call bad cookery is good cookery not good enough for us; what we call a bad civilization is a good civilization not good enough for us. We choose to call the great mass of the history of mankind bad, not because it is bad, but because we are better. This is palpably an unfair principle. Ivory may not be so white as snow, but the whole Arctic continent does not make ivory black.

Now it has appeared to me unfair that humanity should be engaged perpetually in calling all those things bad which have been good enough to make other things better, in everlastingly kicking down the ladder by which it has climbed. It has appeared to me that progress should be something else besides a continual parricide; therefore I have investigated the dust-heaps of humanity, and found a treasure in all of them. I have found that humanity is not incidentally engaged, but eternally and systematically engaged, in throwing gold into the gutter and diamonds into the sea. I have found that every man is disposed to call the green leaf of the tree a little less green than it is, and the snow of Christmas a little less white than it is; therefore I have imagined that the main business of a man, however humble, is defence. I have conceived that a defendant is chiefly required when worldlings despise the world — that a counsel for the defence would not have been out of place in that terrible day when the sun was darkened over Calvary and Man was rejected of men.

A DEFENCE OF PENNY DREADFULS

ONE of the strangest examples of the degree to which ordinary life is undervalued is the example of popular literature, the vast mass of which we contentedly describe as vulgar. The boy's novelette may be ignorant in a literary sense, which is only like saying that a modern novel is ignorant in the chemical sense, or the economic sense, or the astronomical sense; but it is not vulgar intrinsically—it is the actual centre of a million flaming imaginations.

In former centuries the educated class ignored the ruck of vulgar literature. They ignored, and therefore did not, properly speaking, despise it. Simple ignorance and indifference does not inflate the character with pride. A man does not walk down the street giving a haughty twirl to his moustaches at the thought of his superiority to some variety of deep-sea fishes. The old scholars left the whole under-world of popular compositions in a similar darkness.

To-day, however, we have reversed this principle. We do despise vulgar compositions, and we do not ignore them. We are in some danger of becoming petty in our study of pettiness; there is a terrible Circean law in the background that if the soul stoops too ostentatiously to examine anything it never gets up again. There is no class of vulgar publications about which there is, to my mind, more utterly ridiculous exaggeration and misconception than the current boys' literature of the lowest stratum. This class of composition has presumably always existed, and must exist. It has no more claim to be good literature than the daily conversation of its readers to be fine oratory, or the lodging-houses and tenements they inhabit to be sublime architecture. But people must have conversation, they must have houses, and they must have stories. The simple need for some kind of ideal world in which fictitious persons play an unhampered part is infinitely deeper and older than the rules of good art, and much more important. Every one of us in childhood has constructed such an invisible *dramatis personæ*, but it never occurred to our nurses to correct the composition by careful comparison with Balzac. In the East the professional story-teller goes from village to village with a small carpet; and I wish sincerely that anyone had the moral courage to spread that carpet and sit on it in Ludgate Circus. But it is not probable that all the tales of the carpet-bearer are little gems of original artistic workmanship. Literature and fiction are two entirely different things. Literature is a luxury; fiction is a necessity. A work of art can hardly be too short, for its climax is its merit. A story can never be too long, for its conclusion is merely to be deplored, like the last halfpenny or the last pipelight. And so, while the increase of the artistic conscience tends in more ambitious works to brevity and impressionism, voluminous industry still marks the producer of the true romantic trash. There was no end to the ballads of Robin Hood; there is no end to the volumes about Dick Deadshot and the Avenging Nine. These two heroes are deliberately conceived as immortal.

But instead of basing all discussion of the problem upon the common-sense recognition of this fact—that the youth of the lower orders always has had and always must have formless and endless romantic reading of some kind, and then going on to make provision for its wholesomeness—we begin, generally speaking, by fantastic abuse of this reading as a whole and indignant surprise that the errand-boys under discussion do not read 'The Egoist' and 'The Master Builder.' It is the custom, particularly among magistrates, to attribute half the crimes of the Metropolis to cheap novelettes. If some grimy urchin runs away with an apple, the magistrate shrewdly points out that the child's knowledge that apples appease hunger is traceable to some curious literary researches. The boys themselves, when penitent, frequently accuse the novelettes with great bitterness, which is only to be expected from young people possessed of no little native humour. If I had forged a will, and could obtain sympathy by tracing the incident to the influence of Mr. George Moore's novels, I should find the greatest entertainment in the diversion. At any rate, it is firmly fixed in the minds of most people that gutter-boys, unlike everybody else in the community, find their principal motives for conduct in printed books.

Now it is quite clear that this objection, the objection brought by magistrates, has nothing to do with literary merit. Bad story writing is not a crime. Mr. Hall Caine walks the streets openly, and cannot be put in prison for an anticlimax. The objection rests upon the theory that the tone of the mass of boys' novelettes is criminal and degraded, appealing to low cupidity and low cruelty. This is the magisterial theory, and this is rubbish.

So far as I have seen them, in connection with the dirtiest book-stalls in the poorest districts, the facts are simply these: The whole bewildering mass of vulgar juvenile literature is concerned with adventures, rambling, disconnected and endless. It does not express any passion of any sort, for there is no human character of any sort. It runs eternally in certain grooves of local and historical type: the medieval knight, the eighteenth-century duellist, and the modern cowboy, recur with the same stiff simplicity as the conventional human figures in an Oriental pattern. I can quite as easily imagine a human being kindling wild appetites by the contemplation of his Turkey carpet as by such dehumanized and naked narrative as this.

Among these stories there are a certain number which deal sympathetically with the adventures of robbers, outlaws and pirates, which present in a dignified and romantic light thieves and murderers like Dick Turpin and Claude Duval. That is to say, they do precisely the same thing as Scott's 'Ivanhoe,' Scott's 'Rob Roy,' Scott's 'Lady of the Lake,' Byron's 'Corsair,' Wordsworth's 'Rob Roy's Grave,' Stevenson's 'Macaire,' Mr. Max Pemberton's 'Iron Pirate,' and a thousand more works distributed systematically as prizes and Christmas presents. Nobody imagines that an admiration of Locksley in 'Ivanhoe' will lead a boy to shoot Japanese arrows at the deer in Richmond Park; no one thinks that the incautious opening of Wordsworth at the poem on Rob Roy will set him up for life as a blackmailer. In the case of our own class, we recognise that this wild life is contemplated with pleasure by the young, not because it is like their own life, but because it is different from it. It might at least cross our minds that, for whatever other reason the errand-boy reads 'The Red Revenge,' it really is not because he is dripping with the gore of his own friends and relatives.

In this matter, as in all such matters, we lose our bearings entirely by speaking of the 'lower classes' when we mean humanity minus ourselves. This trivial romantic literature is not especially plebeian: it is simply human. The philanthropist can never forget classes and callings. He says, with a modest swagger, 'I have invited twenty-five factory hands to tea.' If he said 'I have invited twenty-five chartered accountants to tea,' everyone would see the humour of so simple a classification. But this is what we have done with this lumberland of foolish writing: we have probed, as if it were some monstrous new disease, what is, in fact, nothing but the foolish and valiant heart of man. Ordinary men will always be sentimentalists: for a sentimentalist is simply a man who has feelings and does not trouble to invent a new way of expressing them. These common and current publications have nothing essentially evil about them. They express the sanguine and heroic truisms on which civilization is built; for it is clear that unless civilization is built on truisms, it is not built at all. Clearly, there could be no safety for a society in which the remark by the Chief Justice that murder was wrong was regarded as an original and dazzling epigram.

If the authors and publishers of 'Dick Deadshot,' and such remarkable works, were suddenly to make a raid upon the educated class, were to take down the names of every man, however distinguished, who was caught at a University Extension Lecture, were to confiscate all our novels and warn us all to correct our lives, we should be seriously annoyed. Yet they have far more right to do so than we; for they, with all their idiotcy, are normal and we are abnormal. It is the modern literature of the educated, not of the uneducated, which is avowedly and aggressively criminal. Books recommending profligacy and pessimism, at which the high-souled errand-boy would shudder, lie upon all our drawing-room tables. If the dirtiest old owner of the dirtiest old bookstall in Whitechapel dared to display works really recommending polygamy or suicide, his stock would be seized by the police. These things are our luxuries. And with a hypocrisy so ludicrous as to be almost unparalleled in history, we rate the gutter-boys for their immorality at the very time that we are discussing (with equivocal German Professors) whether morality is valid at all. At the very instant that we curse the Penny Dreadful for encouraging thefts upon property, we canvass the proposition that all property is theft. At the very instant we accuse it (quite unjustly) of lubricity and indecency, we are cheerfully reading philosophies which glory in lubricity and indecency. At the very instant that we charge it with encouraging the young to destroy life, we are placidly discussing whether life is worth preserving.

But it is we who are the morbid exceptions; it is we who are the criminal class. This should be our great comfort. The vast mass of humanity, with their vast mass of idle books and idle words, have never doubted and never will doubt that courage is splendid, that fidelity is noble, that distressed ladies should be rescued, and vanquished enemies spared. There are a large number of cultivated persons who doubt these maxims of daily life, just as there are a large number of persons who believe they are the Prince of Wales; and I am told that both classes of people are entertaining conversationalists. But the average man or boy writes daily in these great gaudy diaries of his soul, which we call Penny Dreadfuls, a plainer and better gospel than any of those iridescent ethical paradoxes that the fashionable change as often as their bonnets. It may be a very limited aim in morality to shoot a 'many-faced and fickle traitor,' but at least it is a better aim than to be a many-faced and fickle traitor, which is a simple summary of a good many modern systems from Mr. d'Annunzio's downwards. So long as the coarse and thin texture of mere current popular romance is not touched by a paltry culture it will never be vitally immoral. It is always on the side of life. The poor —the slaves who really stoop under the burden of life—have often been mad, scatter-brained and cruel, but never hopeless. That is a class privilege, like cigars. Their drivelling literature will always be a 'blood and thunder' literature, as simple as the thunder of heaven and the blood of men.

A DEFENCE OF RASH VOWS

IF a prosperous modern man, with a high hat and a frock-coat, were to solemnly pledge himself before all his clerks and friends to count the leaves on every third tree in Holland Walk, to hop up to the City on one leg every Thursday, to repeat the whole of Mill's 'Liberty' seventy-six times, to collect 300 dandelions in fields belonging to anyone of the name of Brown, to remain for thirty-one hours holding his left ear in his right hand, to sing the names of all his aunts in order of age on the top of an omnibus, or make any such unusual undertaking, we should immediately conclude that the man was mad, or, as it is sometimes expressed, was 'an artist in life.' Yet these vows are not more extraordinary than the vows which in the Middle Ages and in similar periods were made, not by fanatics merely, but by the greatest figures in civic and national civilization—by kings, judges, poets, and priests. One man swore to chain two mountains together, and the great chain hung there, it was said, for ages as a monument of that mystical folly. Another swore that he would find his way to Jerusalem with a patch over his eyes, and died looking for it. It is not easy to see that these two exploits, judged from a strictly rational standpoint, are any saner than the acts above suggested. A mountain is commonly a stationary and reliable object which it is not necessary to chain up at night like a dog. And it is not easy at first sight to see that a man pays a very high compliment to the Holy City by setting out for it under conditions which render it to the last degree improbable that he will ever get there.

But about this there is one striking thing to be noticed. If men behaved in that way in our time, we should, as we have said, regard them as symbols of the 'decadence.' But the men who did these things were not decadent; they belonged generally to the most robust classes of what is generally regarded as a robust age. Again, it will be urged that if men essentially sane performed such insanities, it was under the capricious direction of a superstitious religious system. This, again, will not hold water; for in the purely terrestrial and even sensual departments of life, such as love and lust, the medieval princes show the same mad promises and performances, the same misshapen imagination and the same monstrous self-sacrifice. Here we have a contradiction, to explain which it is necessary to think of the whole nature of vows from the beginning. And if we consider seriously and correctly the nature of vows, we shall, unless I am much mistaken, come to the conclusion that it is perfectly sane, and even sensible, to swear to chain mountains together, and that, if insanity is involved at all, it is a little insane not to do so.

The man who makes a vow makes an appointment with himself at some distant time or place. The danger of it is that himself should not keep the appointment. And in modern times this terror of one's self, of the weakness and mutability of one's self, has perilously increased, and is the real basis of the objection to vows of any kind. A modern man refrains from swearing to count the leaves on every third tree in Holland Walk, not because it is silly to do so (he does many sillier things), but because he has a profound conviction that before he had got to the three hundred and seventy-ninth leaf on the first tree he would be excessively tired of the subject and want to go home to tea. In other words, we fear that by that time he will be, in the common but hideously significant phrase, *another man.* Now, it is this horrible fairy tale of a man constantly changing into other men that is the soul of the decadence. That John Paterson should, with apparent calm, look forward to being a certain General Barker on Monday, Dr. Macgregor on Tuesday, Sir Walter Carstairs on Wednesday, and Sam Slugg on Thursday, may seem a nightmare; but to that nightmare we give the name of modern culture. One great decadent, who is now dead, published a poem some time ago, in which he powerfully summed up the whole spirit of the movement by declaring that he could stand in the prison yard and entirely comprehend the feelings of a man about to be hanged:

> 'For he that lives more lives than one
> More deaths than one must die.'

And the end of all this is that maddening horror of unreality which descends upon the decadents, and compared with which physical pain itself would have the freshness of a youthful thing. The one hell which imagination must conceive as most hellish is to be eternally acting a play without even the narrowest and dirtiest greenroom in which to be human. And this is the condition of the decadent, of the æsthete, of the free-lover. To be everlastingly passing through dangers which we know cannot scathe us, to be taking oaths which we know cannot bind us, to be defying enemies who we know cannot conquer us—this is the grinning tyranny of decadence which is called freedom.

Let us turn, on the other hand, to the maker of vows. The man who made a vow, however wild, gave a healthy and natural expression to the greatness of a great moment. He vowed, for example, to chain two mountains together, perhaps a symbol of some great relief, or love, or aspiration. Short as the moment of his resolve might be, it was, like all great moments, a moment of immortality, and the desire to say of it *exegi monumentum ære perennius* was the only sentiment that would satisfy his mind. The modern æsthetic man would, of course, easily see the emotional opportunity; he would vow to chain two mountains together. But, then, he would quite as cheerfully vow to chain the earth to the moon. And the withering consciousness that he did not mean what he said, that he was, in truth, saying nothing of any great import, would take from him exactly that sense of daring actuality which is the excitement of a vow. For what could be more maddening than an existence in which our mother or aunt received the information that we were going to assassinate the King or build a temple on Ben Nevis with the genial composure of custom?

The revolt against vows has been carried in our day even to the extent of a revolt against the typical vow of marriage. It is most amusing to listen to the opponents of marriage on this subject. They appear to imagine that the ideal of constancy was a yoke mysteriously imposed on mankind by the devil, instead of being, as it is, a yoke consistently imposed by all lovers on themselves. They have invented a phrase, a phrase that is a black and white contradiction in two words—'free-love'—as if a lover ever had been, or ever could be, free. It is the nature of love to bind itself, and the institution of marriage merely paid the average man the compliment of taking him at his word. Modern sages offer to the lover, with an ill-flavoured grin, the largest liberties and the fullest irresponsibility; but they do not respect him as the old Church respected him; they do not write his oath upon the heavens, as the record of his highest moment. They give him every liberty except the liberty to sell his liberty, which is the only one that he wants.

In Mr. Bernard Shaw's brilliant play 'The Philanderer,' we have a vivid picture of this state of things. Charteris is a man perpetually endeavouring to be a free-lover, which is like endeavouring to be a married bachelor or a white negro. He is wandering in a hungry search for a certain exhilaration which he can only have when he has the courage to cease from wandering. Men knew better than this in old times—in the time, for example, of Shakespeare's heroes. When Shakespeare's men are really celibate they praise the undoubted advantages of celibacy, liberty, irresponsibility, a chance of continual change. But they were not such fools as to continue to talk of liberty when they were in such a condition that they could be made happy or miserable by the moving of someone else's eyebrow. Suckling classes love with debt in his praise of freedom.

> 'And he that's fairly out of both
> Of all the world is blest.
> He lives as in the golden age,
> When all things made were common;
> He takes his pipe, he takes his glass,
> He fears no man or woman.'

This is a perfectly possible, rational and manly position. But what have lovers to do with ridiculous affectations of fearing no man or woman? They know that in the turning of a hand the whole cosmic engine to the remotest star may become an instrument of music or an instrument of torture. They hear a song older than Suckling's, that has survived a hundred philosophies. 'Who is this that looketh out of the window, fair as the sun, clear as the moon, terrible as an army with banners?'

As we have said, it is exactly this back-door, this sense of having a retreat behind us, that is, to our minds, the sterilizing spirit in modern pleasure. Everywhere there is the persistent and insane attempt to obtain pleasure without paying for it. Thus, in politics the modern Jingoes practically say, 'Let us have the pleasures of conquerors without the pains of soldiers: let us sit on sofas and be a hardy race.' Thus, in religion and morals, the decadent mystics say: 'Let us have the fragrance of sacred purity without the sorrows of self-restraint; let us sing hymns alternately to the Virgin and Priapus.' Thus in love the free-lovers say: 'Let us have the splendour of offering ourselves without the peril of committing ourselves; let us see whether one cannot commit suicide an unlimited number of times.'

Emphatically it will not work. There are thrilling moments, doubtless, for the spectator, the amateur, and the æsthete; but there is one thrill that is known only to the soldier who fights for his own flag, to the ascetic who starves himself for his own illumination, to the lover who makes finally his own choice. And it is this transfiguring self-discipline that makes the vow a truly sane thing. It must have satisfied even the giant hunger of the soul of a lover or a poet to know that in consequence of some one instant of decision that strange chain would hang for centuries in the Alps among the silences of stars and snows. All around us is the city of small sins, abounding in backways and retreats, but surely, sooner or later, the towering flame will rise from the harbour announcing that the reign of the cowards is over and a man is burning his ships.

A DEFENCE OF SKELETONS

SOME little time ago I stood among immemorial English trees that seemed to take hold upon the stars like a brood of Ygdrasils. As I walked among these living pillars I became gradually aware that the rustics who lived and died in their shadow adopted a very curious conversational tone. They seemed to be constantly apologizing for the trees, as if they were a very poor show. After elaborate investigation, I discovered that their gloomy and penitent tone was traceable to the fact that it was winter and all the trees were bare. I assured them that I did not resent the fact that it was winter, that I knew the thing had happened before, and that no forethought on their part could have averted this blow of destiny. But I could not in any way reconcile them to the fact that it *was* winter. There was evidently a general feeling that I had caught the trees in a kind of disgraceful deshabille, and that they ought not to be seen until, like the first human sinners, they had covered themselves with leaves. So it is quite clear that, while very few people appear to know anything of how trees look in winter, the actual foresters know less than anyone. So far from the line of the tree when it is bare appearing harsh and severe, it is luxuriantly indefinable to an unusual degree; the fringe of the forest melts away like a vignette. The tops of two or three high trees when they are leafless are so soft that they seem like the gigantic brooms of that fabulous lady who was sweeping the cobwebs off the sky. The outline of a leafy forest is in comparison hard, gross and blotchy; the clouds of night do not more certainly obscure the moon than those green and monstrous clouds obscure the tree; the actual sight of the little wood, with its gray and silver sea of life, is entirely a winter vision. So dim and delicate is the heart of the winter woods, a kind of glittering gloaming, that a figure stepping towards us in the chequered twilight seems as if he were breaking through unfathomable depths of spiders' webs.

But surely the idea that its leaves are the chief grace of a tree is a vulgar one, on a par with the idea that his hair is the chief grace of a pianist. When winter, that healthy ascetic, carries his gigantic razor over hill and valley, and shaves all the trees like monks, we feel surely that they are all the more like trees if they are shorn, just as so many painters and musicians would be all the more like men if they were less like mops. But it does appear to be a deep and essential difficulty that men have an abiding terror of their own structure, or of the structure of things they love. This is felt dimly in the skeleton of the tree: it is felt profoundly in the skeleton of the man.

The importance of the human skeleton is very great, and the horror with which it is commonly regarded is somewhat mysterious. Without claiming for the human skeleton a wholly conventional beauty, we may assert that he is certainly not uglier than a bull-dog, whose popularity never wanes, and that he has a vastly more cheerful and ingratiating expression. But just as man is mysteriously ashamed of the skeletons of the trees in winter, so he is mysteriously ashamed of the skeleton of himself in death. It is a singular thing altogether, this horror of the architecture of things. One would think it would be most unwise in a man to be afraid of a skeleton, since Nature has set curious and quite insuperable obstacles to his running away from it.

One ground exists for this terror: a

strange idea has infected humanity that the skeleton is typical of death. A man might as well say that a factory chimney was typical of bankruptcy. The factory may be left naked after ruin, the skeleton may be left naked after bodily dissolution; but both of them have had a lively and workmanlike life of their own, all the pulleys creaking, all the wheels turning, in the House of Livelihood as in the House of Life. There is no reason why this creature (new, as I fancy, to art), the living skeleton, should not become the essential symbol of life.

The truth is that man's horror of the skeleton is not horror of death at all. It is man's eccentric glory that he has not, generally speaking, any objection to being dead, but has a very serious objection to being undignified. And the fundamental matter which troubles him in the skeleton is the reminder that the ground-plan of his appearance is shamelessly grotesque. I do not know why he should object to this. He contentedly takes his place in a world that does not pretend to be genteel—a laughing, working, jeering world. He sees millions of animals carrying, with quite a dandified levity, the most monstrous shapes and appendages, the most preposterous horns, wings, and legs, when they are necessary to utility. He sees the good temper of the frog, the unaccountable happiness of the hippopotamus. He sees a whole universe which is ridiculous, from the animalcule, with a head too big for its body, up to the comet, with a tail too big for its head. But when it comes to the delightful oddity of his own inside, his sense of humour rather abruptly deserts him.

In the Middle Ages and in the Renaissance (which was, in certain times and respects, a much gloomier period) this idea of the skeleton had a vast influence in freezing the pride out of all earthly pomps and the fragrance out of all fleeting pleasures. But it was not, surely, the mere dread of death that did this, for these were ages in which men went to meet death singing; it was the idea of the degradation of man in the grinning ugliness of his structure that withered the juvenile insolence of beauty and pride. And in this it almost assuredly did more good than harm. There is nothing so cold or so pitiless as youth, and youth in aristocratic stations and ages tended to an impeccable dignity, an endless summer of success which needed to be very sharply reminded of the scorn of the stars. It was well that such flamboyant prigs should be convinced that one practical joke, at least, would bowl them over, that they would fall into one grinning man-trap, and not rise again. That the whole structure of their existence was as wholesomely ridiculous as that of a pig or a parrot they could not be expected to realize; that birth was humorous, coming of age humorous, drinking and fighting humorous, they were far too young and solemn to know. But at least they were taught that death was humorous.

There is a peculiar idea abroad that the value and fascination of what we call Nature lie in her beauty. But the fact that Nature is beautiful in the sense that a dado or a Liberty curtain is beautiful, is only one of her charms, and almost an accidental one. The highest and most valuable quality in Nature is not her beauty, but her generous and defiant ugliness. A hundred instances might be taken. The croaking noise of the rooks is, in itself, as hideous as the whole hell of sounds in a London railway tunnel. Yet it uplifts us like a trumpet with its coarse kindliness and honesty, and the lover in 'Maud' could actually persuade himself that this abominable noise resembled his lady-love's name. Has the poet, for whom Nature means only roses and lilies, ever heard a pig grunting?

It is a noise that does a man good—a strong, snorting, imprisoned noise, breaking its way out of unfathomable dungeons through every possible outlet and organ. It might be the voice of the earth itself, snoring in its mighty sleep. This is the deepest, the oldest, the most wholesome and religious sense of the value of Nature—the value which comes from her immense babyishness. She is as top-heavy, as grotesque, as solemn and as happy as a child. The mood does come when we see all her shapes like shapes that a baby scrawls upon a slate—simple, rudimentary, a million years older and stronger than the whole disease that is called Art. The objects of earth and heaven seem to combine into a nursery tale, and our relation to things seems for a moment so simple that a dancing lunatic would be needed to do justice to its lucidity and levity. The tree above my head is flapping like some gigantic bird standing on one leg; the moon is like the eye of a cyclops. And, however much my face clouds with sombre vanity, or vulgar vengeance, or contemptible contempt, the bones of my skull beneath it are laughing for ever.

A DEFENCE OF PUBLICITY

IT is a very significant fact that the form of art in which the modern world has certainly not improved upon the ancient is what may roughly be called the art of the open air. Public monuments have certainly not improved, nor has the criticism of them improved, as is evident from the fashion of condemning such a large number of them as pompous. An interesting essay might be written on the enormous number of words that are used as insults when they are really compliments. It is in itself a singular study in that tendency which, as I have said, is always making things out worse than they are, and necessitating a systematic attitude of defence. Thus, for example, some dramatic critics cast contempt upon a dramatic performance by calling it theatrical, which simply means that it is suitable to a theatre, and is as much a compliment as calling a poem poetical. Similarly we speak disdainfully of a certain kind of work as sentimental, which simply means possessing the admirable and essential quality of sentiment. Such phrases are all parts of one peddling and cowardly philosophy, and remind us of the days when 'enthusiast' was a term of reproach. But of all this vocabulary of unconscious eulogies nothing is more striking than the word 'pompous.'

Properly speaking, of course, a public monument ought to be pompous. Pomp is its very object; it would be absurd to have columns and pyramids blushing in some coy nook like violets in the woods of spring. And public monuments have in this matter a great and much-needed lesson to teach. Valour and mercy and the great enthusiasms ought to be a great deal more public than they are at present. We are too fond nowadays of committing the sin of fear and calling it the virtue of reverence. We have forgotten the old and wholesome morality of the Book of Proverbs, 'Wisdom crieth without; her voice is heard in the streets.' In Athens and Florence her voice was heard in the streets. They had an outdoor life of war and argument, and they had what modern commercial civilization has never had—an outdoor art. Religious services, the most sacred of all things, have always been held publicly; it is entirely a new and debased notion that sanctity is the same as secrecy.

A great many modern poets, with the most abstruse and delicate sensibilities, love darkness, when all is said and done, much for the same reason that thieves love it. The mission of a great spire or statue should be to strike the spirit with a sudden sense of pride as with a thunderbolt. It should lift us with it into the empty and ennobling air. Along the base of every noble monument, whatever else may be written there, runs in invisible letters the lines of Swinburne :

> 'This thing is God :
> To be man with thy might,
> To go straight in the strength of thy spirit, and live out thy life in the light.'

If a public monument does not meet this first supreme and obvious need, that it should be public and monumental, it fails from the outset.

There has arisen lately a school of realistic sculpture, which may perhaps be better described as a school of sketchy sculpture. Such a movement was right and inevitable as a reaction from the mean and dingy pomposity of English Victorian statuary. Perhaps the most hideous and depressing object in the universe—far more hideous and depressing than one of Mr. H. G. Wells's shapeless monsters of the slime (and not at all unlike them)—is the statue of an English philanthropist. Almost as bad, though, of course, not quite as bad, are the statues of English politicians in Parliament Fields. Each of them is cased in a cylindrical frock-coat, and each carries either a scroll or a dubious-looking garment over the arm that might be either a bathing-towel or a light great-coat. Each of them is in an oratorical attitude, which has all the disadvantage of being affected without even any of the advantages of being theatrical. Let no one suppose that such abortions arise merely from technical demerit. In every line of those leaden dolls is expressed the fact that they were not set up with any heat of natural enthusiasm for beauty or dignity. They were set up mechanically, because it would seem indecorous or stingy if they were not set up. They were even set up sulkily, in a utilitarian age which was haunted by the thought that there were a great many more sensible ways of spending money. So long as this is the dominant national sentiment, the land is barren, statues and churches will not grow—for they have to grow, as much as trees and flowers. But this moral disadvantage which lay so heavily upon the early Victorian sculpture lies in a modified degree upon that rough, picturesque, commonplace sculpture which has begun to arise, and of which the statue of Darwin in the South Kensington Museum and the statue of Gordon in Trafalgar Square are admirable examples. It is not enough for a popular monument to be artistic, like a black charcoal sketch ; it must be striking; it must be in the highest sense of the word sensational; it must stand for humanity; it must speak for us to the stars ; it must declare in the face of all the heavens that when the longest and blackest catalogue has been made of all our crimes and follies there are some things of which we men are not ashamed.

The two modes of commemorating a public man are a statue and a biography. They are alike in certain respects, as, for example, in the fact that neither of them resembles the original, and that both of them commonly tone down not only all a man's vices, but all the more amusing of his virtues. But they are treated in one respect differently. We never hear anything about biography without hearing something about the sanctity of private life and the necessity for suppressing the whole of the most important part of a man's existence. The sculptor does not work at this disadvantage. The sculptor does not leave out the nose of an eminent philanthropist because it is too beautiful to be given to the public; he does not depict a statesman with a sack over his head because his smile was too sweet to be endurable in the light of day. But in biography the thesis is popularly and solidly maintained, so that it requires some courage even to hint a doubt of it, that the better a man was, the more truly human life he led, the less should be said about it.

For this idea, this modern idea that sanctity is identical with secrecy, there is one thing at least to be said. It is for all practical purposes an entirely new idea; it was unknown to all the ages in which the idea of sanctity really flourished. The record of the great spiritual movements of mankind is dead against the idea that spirituality is a private matter. The most awful secret of every man's soul, its most lonely and individual need, its most primal and psychological relationship, the thing called worship, the communication between the soul and the last reality—this most private matter is the most public spectacle in the world. Anyone who chooses to walk into a large church on Sunday morning may see a hundred men each alone with his Maker. He stands, in truth, in the presence of one of the strangest spectacles in the world—a mob of hermits. And in thus definitely espousing publicity by making public the most internal mystery, Christianity acts in accordance with its earliest origins and its terrible beginning. It was surely by no accident that the spectacle which darkened the sun at noonday was set upon a hill. The martyrdoms of the early Christians were public not only by the caprice of the oppressor, but by the whole desire and conception of the victims.

The mere grammatical meaning of the word 'martyr' breaks into pieces at a blow the whole notion of the privacy of goodness. The Christian martyrdoms were more than demonstrations: they were advertisements. In our day the new theory of spiritual delicacy would desire to alter all this. It would permit Christ to be crucified if it was necessary to His Divine nature, but it would ask in the name of good taste why He could not be crucified in a private room. It would declare that the act of a martyr in being torn in pieces by lions was vulgar and sensational, though, of course, it would have no objection to being torn in pieces by a lion in one's own parlour before a circle of really intimate friends.

It is, I am inclined to think, a decadent and diseased purity which has inaugurated this notion that the sacred object must be hidden. The stars have never lost their sanctity, and they are more shameless and naked and numerous than advertisements of Pears' soap. It would be a strange world indeed if Nature was suddenly stricken with this ethereal shame, if the trees grew with their roots in the air and their load of leaves and blossoms underground, if the flowers closed at dawn and opened at sunset, if the sunflower turned towards the darkness, and the birds flew, like bats, by night.

A DEFENCE OF NONSENSE

THERE are two equal and eternal ways of looking at this twilight world of ours: we may see it as the twilight of evening or the twilight of morning; we may think of anything, down to a fallen acorn, as a descendant or as an ancestor. There are times when we are almost crushed, not so much with the load of the evil as with the load of the goodness of humanity, when we feel that we are nothing but the inheritors of a humiliating splendour. But there are other times when everything seems primitive, when the ancient stars are only sparks blown from a boy's bonfire, when the whole earth seems so young and experimental that even the white hair of the aged, in the fine biblical phrase, is like almond-trees that blossom, like the white hawthorn grown in May. That it is good for a man to realize that he is 'the heir of all the ages' is pretty commonly admitted; it is a less popular but equally important point that it is good for him sometimes to realize that he is not only an ancestor, but an ancestor of primal antiquity; it is good for him to wonder whether he is not a hero, and to experience ennobling doubts as to whether he is not a solar myth.

The matters which most thoroughly evoke this sense of the abiding childhood of the world are those which are really fresh, abrupt and inventive in any age; and if we were asked what was the best proof of this adventurous youth in the nineteenth century we should say, with all respect to its portentous sciences and philosophies, that it was to be found in the rhymes of Mr. Edward Lear and in the literature of nonsense. 'The Dong with the Luminous Nose,' at least, is original, as the first ship and the first plough were original.

It is true in a certain sense that some of the greatest writers the world has seen—Aristophanes, Rabelais and Sterne—have written nonsense; but unless we are mistaken, it is in a widely different sense. The nonsense of these men was satiric—that is to say, symbolic; it was a kind of exuberant capering round a discovered truth. There is all the difference in the world between the instinct of satire, which, seeing in the Kaiser's moustaches something typical of him, draws them continually larger and larger; and the instinct of nonsense which, for no reason whatever, imagines what those moustaches would look like on the present Archbishop of Canterbury if he grew them in a fit of absence of mind. We incline to think that no age except our own could have understood that the Quangle-Wangle meant absolutely nothing, and the Lands of the Jumblies were absolutely nowhere. We fancy that if the account of the knave's trial in 'Alice in Wonderland' had been published in the seventeenth century it would have been bracketed with Bunyan's 'Trial of Faithful' as a parody on the State prosecutions of the time. We fancy that if 'The Dong with the Luminous Nose' had appeared in the same period everyone would have called it a dull satire on Oliver Cromwell.

It is altogether advisedly that we quote chiefly from Mr. Lear's 'Nonsense Rhymes.' To our mind he is both chronologically and essentially the father of nonsense; we think him superior to Lewis Carroll. In one sense, indeed, Lewis Carroll has a great advantage. We know what Lewis Carroll was in daily life: he was a singularly serious and conventional don, universally respected, but very much of a pedant and something of a Philistine. Thus his strange double life in earth and in dreamland emphasizes the idea that lies at the back of nonsense—the idea of *escape*, of escape into a world where things are not fixed horribly in an eternal appropriateness, where apples grow on pear-trees, and any odd man you meet may have three legs. Lewis Carroll, living one life in which he would have thundered morally against any one who walked on the wrong plot of grass, and another life in which he would cheerfully call the sun green and the moon blue, was, by his very divided nature, his one foot on both worlds, a perfect type of the position of modern nonsense. His Wonderland is a country populated by insane mathematicians. We feel the whole is an escape into a world of masquerade; we feel that if we could pierce their disguises, we might discover that Humpty Dumpty and the March Hare were Professors and Doctors of Divinity enjoying a mental holiday. This sense of escape is certainly less emphatic in Edward Lear, because of the completeness of his citizenship in the world of unreason. We do not know his prosaic biography as we know Lewis Carroll's. We accept him as a purely fabulous figure, on his own description of himself:

> 'His body is perfectly spherical,
> He weareth a runcible hat.'

While Lewis Carroll's Wonderland is

purely intellectual, Lear introduces quite another element — the element of the poetical and even emotional. Carroll works by the pure reason, but this is not so strong a contrast; for, after all, mankind in the main has always regarded reason as a bit of a joke. Lear introduces his unmeaning words and his amorphous creatures not with the pomp of reason, but with the romantic prelude of rich hues and haunting rhythms.

> 'Far and few, far and few,
> Are the lands where the Jumblies live,'

is an entirely different type of poetry to that exhibited in 'Jabberwocky.' Carroll, with a sense of mathematical neatness, makes his whole poem a mosaic of new and mysterious words. But Edward Lear, with more subtle and placid effrontery, is always introducing scraps of his own elvish dialect into the middle of simple and rational statements, until we are almost stunned into admitting that we know what they mean. There is a genial ring of commonsense about such lines as,

> 'For his aunt Jobiska said "Every one knows
> That a Pobble is better without his toes,"'

which is beyond the reach of Carroll. The

poet seems so easy on the matter that we are almost driven to pretend that we see his meaning, that we know the peculiar difficulties of a Pobble, that we are as old travellers in the 'Gromboolian Plain' as he is.

Our claim that nonsense is a new literature (we might almost say a new sense) would be quite indefensible if nonsense were nothing more than a mere æsthetic fancy. Nothing sublimely artistic has ever arisen out of mere art, any more than anything essentially reasonable has ever arisen out of the pure reason. There must always be a rich moral soil for any great æsthetic growth. The principle of *art for art's sake* is a very good principle if it means that there is a vital distinction between the earth and the tree that has its roots in the earth; but it is a very bad principle if it means that the tree could grow just as well with its roots in the air. Every great literature has always been allegorical—allegorical of some view of the whole universe. The 'Iliad' is only great because all life is a battle, the 'Odyssey' because all life is a journey, the Book of Job because all life is a riddle. There is one attitude in which we think that all existence is summed up in the word 'ghosts'; another, and somewhat better one, in which we think it is summed up in the words 'A Midsummer Night's Dream.' Even the vulgarest melodrama or detective story can be good if it expresses something of the delight in sinister possibilities—the healthy lust for darkness and terror which may come on us any night in walking down a dark lane. If, therefore, nonsense is really to be the literature of the future, it must have its own version of the Cosmos to offer; the world must not only be the tragic, romantic, and religious, it must be nonsensical also. And here we fancy that nonsense will, in a very unexpected way, come to the aid of the spiritual view of things. Religion has for centuries been trying to make men exult in the 'wonders' of creation, but it has forgotten that a thing cannot be completely wonderful so long as it remains sensible. So long as we regard a tree as an obvious thing, naturally and reasonably created for a giraffe to eat, we cannot properly wonder at it. It is when we consider it as a prodigious wave of the living soil sprawling up to the skies for no reason in particular that we take off our hats, to the astonishment of the park-keeper. Everything has in fact another side to it, like the moon, the patroness of nonsense. Viewed from that other side, a bird is a blossom broken loose from its chain of stalk, a man a quadruped begging on its hind legs, a house a gigantesque hat to cover a man from the sun, a chair an apparatus of four wooden legs for a cripple with only two.

This is the side of things which tends most truly to spiritual wonder. It is significant that in the greatest religious poem existent, the Book of Job, the argument which convinces the infidel is not (as has been represented by the merely rational religionism of the eighteenth century) a picture of the ordered beneficence of the Creation; but, on the contrary, a picture of the huge and undecipherable unreason of it. 'Hast Thou sent the rain upon the desert where no man is?' This simple sense of wonder at the shapes of things, and at their exuberant independence of our intellectual standards and our trivial definitions, is the basis of spirituality as it is the basis of nonsense. Nonsense and faith (strange as the conjunction may seem) are the two supreme symbolic assertions of the truth that to draw out the soul of things with a syllogism is as impossible as to draw out Leviathan with a hook. The well-meaning person who, by merely studying the logical side of things, has decided that 'faith is nonsense,' does not know how truly he speaks; later it may come back to him in the form that nonsense is faith.

A DEFENCE OF PLANETS

A BOOK has at one time come under my notice called 'Terra Firma: the Earth not a Planet.' The author was a Mr. D. Wardlaw Scott, and he quoted very seriously the opinions of a large number of other persons, of whom we have never heard, but who are evidently very important. Mr. Beach of Southsea, for example, thinks that the world is flat; and in Southsea perhaps it is. It is no part of my present intention, however, to follow Mr. Scott's arguments in detail. On the lines of such arguments it may be shown that the earth is flat, and, for the matter of that, that it is triangular. A few examples will suffice:

One of Mr. Scott's objections was that if a projectile is fired from a moving body there is a difference in the distance to which it carries according to the direction in which it is sent. But as in practice there is not the slightest difference whichever way the thing is done, in the case of the earth 'we have a forcible overthrow of all fancies relative to the motion of the earth, and a striking proof that the earth is not a globe.'

This is altogether one of the quaintest arguments we have ever seen. It never seems to occur to the author, among other things, that when the firing and falling of the shot all take place upon the moving body, there is nothing whatever to compare them with. As a matter of fact, of course, a shot fired at an elephant does actually often travel towards the marksman, but much slower than the marksman travels. Mr. Scott probably would not like to contemplate the fact that the elephant, properly speaking, swings round and hits the bullet. To us it appears full of a rich cosmic humour.

I will only give one other example of the astronomical proofs :

'If the earth were a globe, the distance round the surface, say, at 45 degrees south latitude, could not possibly be any greater than the same latitude north ; but since it is found by navigators to be twice the distance—to say the least of it—or double the distance it ought to be according to the globular theory, it is a proof that the earth is not a globe.'

This sort of thing reduces my mind to a pulp. I can faintly resist when a man says that if the earth were a globe cats would not have four legs; but when he says that if the earth were a globe cats would not have five legs I am crushed.

But, as I have indicated, it is not in the scientific aspect of this remarkable theory that I am for the moment interested. It is rather with the difference between the flat and the round worlds as conceptions in art and imagination that I am concerned. It is a very remarkable thing that none of us are really Copernicans in our actual outlook upon things. We are convinced intellectually that we inhabit a small provincial planet, but we do not feel in the least suburban. Men of science have quarrelled with the Bible because it is not based upon the true astronomical system, but it is certainly open to the orthodox to say that if it had been it would never have convinced anybody.

If a single poem or a single story were really transfused with the Copernican idea, the thing would be a nightmare. Can we think of a solemn scene of mountain stillness in which some prophet is standing in a trance, and then realize that the whole scene is whizzing round like a zoetrope at the rate of nineteen miles a second? Could we tolerate the notion of a mighty King delivering a sublime fiat and then remember that for all practical purposes he is hanging head downwards in space? A strange fable might be written of a man who was blessed or cursed with the Copernican eye, and saw all men on the earth like tintacks clustering round a magnet. It would be singular to imagine how very different the speech of an aggressive egoist, announcing the independence and divinity of man, would sound if he were seen hanging on to the planet by his boot soles.

For, despite Mr. Wardlaw Scott's horror at the Newtonian astronomy and its contradiction of the Bible, the whole distinction is a good instance of the difference between letter and spirit; the letter of the Old Testament is opposed to the conception of the solar system, but the spirit has much kinship with it. The writers of the Book of Genesis had no theory of gravitation, which to the normal person will appear a fact of as much importance as that they had no umbrellas. But the theory of gravitation has a curiously Hebrew sentiment in it—a sentiment of combined dependence and certainty, a sense of grappling unity, by which all things hang upon one thread. 'Thou hast hanged the world upon nothing,' said the author of the Book of Job, and in that sentence wrote the whole appalling poetry of modern astronomy. The sense of the preciousness and fragility of the universe, the sense of being in the hollow of a hand, is one which the round and rolling earth gives in its most thrilling form. Mr. Wardlaw Scott's flat earth would be the true territory for a comfortable atheist. Nor would the old Jews have any objection to being as much upside down as right way up. They had no foolish ideas about the dignity of man.

It would be an interesting speculation to imagine whether the world will ever develop a Copernican poetry and a Copernican habit of fancy; whether we shall ever speak of 'early earth-turn' instead of 'early sunrise,' and speak indifferently of looking up at the daisies, or looking down on the stars. But if we ever do, there are really a large number of big and fantastic facts awaiting us, worthy to make a new mythology. Mr. Wardlaw Scott, for example, with genuine, if unconscious, imagination, says that according to astronomers, 'the sea is a vast mountain of water miles high.' To have discovered that mountain of moving crystal, in which the fishes build like birds, is like discovering Atlantis: it is enough to make the old world young again. In the new poetry which we contemplate, athletic young men will set out sturdily to climb up the face of the sea. If we once realize all this earth as it is, we should find ourselves in a land of miracles: we shall discover a new planet at the moment that we discover our own. Among all the strange things that men have forgotten, the most universal and catastrophic lapse of memory is that by which they have forgotten that they are living on a star.

In the early days of the world, the discovery of a fact of natural history was immediately followed by the realization of it as a fact of poetry. When man awoke from the long fit of absent-mindedness which is called the automatic animal state, and began to notice the queer facts that the sky was blue and the grass green, he immediately began to use those facts symbolically. Blue, the colour of the sky, became a symbol of celestial holiness; green passed into the language as indicating a freshness verging upon unintelligence. If we had the good fortune to live in a world in which the sky was green and the grass blue, the symbolism would have been different. But for some mysterious reason this habit of realizing poetically the facts of science has ceased abruptly with scientific progress, and all the confounding portents preached by Galileo and Newton have fallen on deaf ears. They painted a picture of the universe compared with which the Apocalypse with its falling stars was a mere idyll. They declared that we are all careering through space, clinging to a cannon-ball, and the poets ignore the matter as if it were a remark about the weather. They say that an invisible force holds us in our own armchairs while the earth hurtles like a boomerang; and men still go back to dusty records to prove the mercy of God. They tell us that Mr. Scott's monstrous vision of a mountain of sea-water rising in a solid dome, like the glass mountain in the fairy-tale, is actually a fact, and men still go back to the fairy-tale. To what towering heights of poetic imagery might we not have risen if only the poetizing of natural history had continued and man's fancy had played with the planets as naturally as it once played with the flowers! We might have had a planetary patriotism, in which the green leaf should be like a cockade, and the sea an everlasting dance of drums. We might have been proud of what our star has wrought, and worn its heraldry haughtily in the blind tournament of the spheres. All this, indeed, we may surely do yet; for with all the multiplicity of knowledge there is one thing happily that no man knows: whether the world is old or young.

A DEFENCE OF CHINA SHEPHERDESSES

THERE are some things of which the world does not like to be reminded, for they are the dead loves of the world. One of these is that great enthusiasm for the Arcadian life which, however much it may now lie open to the sneers of realism, did, beyond all question, hold sway for an enormous period of the world's history, from the times that we describe as ancient down to times that may fairly be called recent. The conception of the innocent and hilarious life of shepherds and shepherdesses certainly covered and absorbed the time of Theocritus, of Virgil, of Catullus, of Dante, of Cervantes, of Ariosto, of Shakespeare, and of Pope. We are told that the gods of the heathen were stone and brass, but stone and brass have never endured with the long endurance of the China Shepherdess. The Catholic Church and the Ideal Shepherd are indeed almost the only things that have bridged the abyss between the ancient world and the modern. Yet, as we say, the world does not like to be reminded of this boyish enthusiasm.

But imagination, the function of the historian, cannot let so great an element alone. By the cheap revolutionary it is commonly supposed that imagination is a merely rebellious thing, that it has its chief function in devising new and fantastic republics. But imagination has its highest use in a retrospective realization. The trumpet of imagination, like the trumpet of the Resurrection, calls the dead out of their graves. Imagination sees Delphi with the eyes of a Greek, Jerusalem with the eyes of a Crusader, Paris with the eyes of a Jacobin, and Arcadia with the eyes of a Euphuist. The prime function of imagination is to see our whole orderly system of life as a pile of stratified revolutions. In spite of all revolutionaries it must be said that the function of imagination is not to make strange things settled, so much as to make settled things strange; not so much to make wonders facts as to make facts wonders. To the imaginative the truisms are all paradoxes, since they were paradoxes in the Stone Age; to them the ordinary copy-book blazes with blasphemy.

Let us, then, consider in this light the old pastoral or Arcadian ideal. But first certainly one thing must be definitely recognised. This Arcadian art and literature is a lost enthusiasm. To study it is like fumbling in the love-letters of a dead man. To us its flowers seem as tawdry as cockades; the lambs that dance to the shepherd's pipe seem to dance with all the artificiality of a ballet. Even our own prosaic toil seems to us more joyous than that holiday. Where its ancient exuberance passed the bounds of wisdom and even of virtue, its caperings seem frozen into the stillness of an antique frieze. In those gray old pictures a bacchanal seems as dull as an archdeacon. Their very sins seem colder than our restraints.

All this may be frankly recognised: all the barren sentimentality of the Arcadian ideal and all its insolent optimism. But when all is said and done, something else remains.

Through ages in which the most arrogant and elaborate ideals of power and civilization held otherwise undisputed sway, the ideal of the perfect and healthy peasant did undoubtedly represent in some shape or form the conception that there was a dignity in simplicity and a dignity in labour. It was good for the ancient aristocrat, even if he could not attain to innocence and the wisdom of the earth, to believe that these things were the secrets of the priesthood of the poor. It was good for him to believe that even if heaven was not above him, heaven was below him. It was well that he should have amid all his flamboyant triumphs the never-extinguished sentiment that there was something better than his triumphs, the conception that 'there remaineth a rest.'

The conception of the Ideal Shepherd seems absurd to our modern ideas. But, after all, it was perhaps the only trade of the democracy which was equalized with the trades of the aristocracy even by the aristocracy itself. The shepherd of pastoral poetry was, without doubt, very different from the shepherd of actual fact. Where one innocently piped to his lambs, the other innocently swore at them; and their divergence in intellect and personal cleanliness was immense. But the difference between the ideal shepherd who danced with Amaryllis and the real shepherd who thrashed her is not a scrap greater than the difference between the ideal soldier who dies to capture the colours and the real soldier who lives to clean his accoutrements, between the ideal priest who is everlastingly by someone's bed and the real priest who is as glad as anyone else to get to his own. There are ideal conceptions and real men in every calling; yet there are few who object to the ideal conceptions, and not many, after all, who object to the real men.

The fact, then, is this: So far from resenting the existence in art and literature of an ideal shepherd, I genuinely regret that the shepherd is the only democratic calling that has ever been raised to the level of the heroic callings conceived by an aristocratic age. So far from objecting to the Ideal Shepherd, I wish there were an Ideal Postman, an Ideal Grocer, and an Ideal Plumber. It is undoubtedly true that we should laugh at the idea of an Ideal Postman; it is true, and it proves that we are not genuine democrats.

Undoubtedly the modern grocer, if called upon to act in an Arcadian manner, if desired to oblige with a symbolic dance expressive of the delights of grocery, or to perform on some simple instrument while his assistants skipped around him, would be embarrassed, and perhaps even reluctant. But it may be questioned whether this temporary reluctance of the grocer is a good thing, or evidence of a good condition of poetic feeling in the grocery business as a whole. There certainly should be an ideal image of health and happiness in any trade, and its remoteness from the reality is not the only important question. No one supposes that the mass of traditional conceptions of duty and glory are always operative, for example, in the mind of a soldier or a doctor ; that the Battle of Waterloo actually makes a private enjoy pipeclaying his trousers, or that the 'health of humanity' softens the momentary phraseology of a physician called out of bed at two o'clock in the morning. But although no ideal obliterates the ugly drudgery and detail of any calling, that ideal does, in the case of the soldier or the doctor, exist definitely in the background and makes that drudgery worth while as a whole. It is a serious calamity that no such ideal exists in the case of the vast number of honourable trades and crafts on which the existence of a modern city depends. It is a pity that current thought and sentiment offer nothing corresponding to the old conception of patron saints. If they did there would be a Patron Saint of Plumbers, and this would alone be a revolution, for it would force the individual craftsman to believe that there was once a perfect being who did actually plumb.

When all is said and done, then, we think it much open to question whether the world has not lost something in the complete disappearance of the ideal of the happy peasant. It is foolish enough to suppose that the rustic went about all over ribbons, but it is better than knowing that he goes about all over rags and being indifferent to the fact. The modern realistic study of the poor does in reality lead the student further astray than the old idyllic notion. For we cannot get the chiaroscuro of humble life so long as its virtues seem to us as gross as its vices and its joys as sullen as its sorrows. Probably at the very moment that we can see nothing but a dull-faced man smoking and drinking heavily with his friend in a pot-house, the man himself is on his soul's holiday, crowned with the flowers of a passionate idleness, and far more like the Happy Peasant than the world will ever know.

A DEFENCE OF USEFUL INFORMATION

IT is natural and proper enough that the masses of explosive ammunition stored up in detective stories and the replete and solid sweet-stuff shops which are called sentimental novelettes should be popular with the ordinary customer. It is not difficult to realize that all of us, ignorant or cultivated, are primarily interested in murder and love-making. The really extraordinary thing is that the most appalling fictions are not actually so popular as that literature which deals with the most undisputed and depressing facts. Men are not apparently so interested in murder and love-making as they are in the number of different forms of latchkey which exist in London or the time that it would take a grasshopper to jump from Cairo to the Cape. The enormous mass of fatuous and useless truth which fills the most widely-circulated papers, such as *Tit-Bits*, *Science Siftings*, and many of the illustrated magazines, is certainly one of the most extraordinary kinds of emotional and mental pabulum on which man ever fed. It is almost incredible that these preposterous statistics should actually be more popular than the most blood-curdling mysteries and the most luxurious debauches of sentiment. To imagine it is like imagining the humorous passages in Bradshaw's Railway Guide read aloud on winter evenings. It is like conceiving a man unable to put down an advertisement of Mother Seigel's Syrup because he wished to know what eventually happened to the young man who was extremely ill at Edinburgh. In the case of cheap detective stories and cheap novelettes, we can most of us feel, whatever our degree of education, that it might be possible to read them if we gave full indulgence to a lower and more facile part of our natures; at the worst we feel that we might enjoy them as we might enjoy bull-baiting or getting drunk. But the literature of information is absolutely mysterious to us. We can no more think of amusing ourselves with it than of reading whole pages of a Surbiton local directory. To read such things would not be a piece of vulgar indulgence; it would be a highly arduous and meritorious enterprise. It is this fact which constitutes a profound and almost unfathomable interest in this particular branch of popular literature.

Primarily, at least, there is one rather peculiar thing which must in justice be said about it. The readers of this strange science must be allowed to be, upon the whole, as disinterested as a prophet seeing visions or a child reading fairy-tales. Here, again, we find, as we so often do, that whatever view of this matter of popular literature we can trust, we can trust least of all the comment and censure current among the vulgar educated. The ordinary version of the ground of this popularity for information, which would be given by a person of greater cultivation, would be that common men are chiefly interested in those sordid facts that surround them on every side. A very small degree of examination will show us that whatever ground there is for the popularity of these insane encyclopædias, it cannot be the ground of utility. The version of life given by a penny novelette may be very moonstruck and unreliable, but it is at least more likely to contain facts relevant to daily life than compilations on the subject of the number of cows' tails that would reach the North Pole. There are many more people who are in love than there are people who have any intention of counting or collecting cows' tails. It is evident to me that the grounds of this widespread madness of information for information's sake must be sought in other and deeper parts of human nature than those daily needs which lie so near the surface that even social philosophers have discovered them somewhere in that profound and eternal instinct for enthusiasm and minding other people's business which made great popular movements like the Crusades or the Gordon Riots.

I once had the pleasure of knowing a man who actually talked in private life after the manner of these papers. His conversation consisted of fragmentary statements about height and weight and depth and time and population, and his conversation was a nightmare of dulness. During the shortest pause he would ask whether his interlocutors were aware how many tons of rust were scraped every year off the Menai Bridge, and how many rival shops Mr. Whiteley had bought up since he opened his business. The attitude of his acquaintances towards this inexhaustible entertainer varied according to his presence or absence between indifference and terror. It was frightful to think of a man's brain being stocked with such inexpressibly profitless treasures. It was like visiting some imposing British Museum and finding its galleries and glass cases filled with specimens of London mud, of common mortar, of broken walking-sticks and cheap tobacco. Years afterwards I discovered that this intolerable prosaic bore had been, in fact, a poet. I learnt that every item of this multitudinous information was totally and unblushingly untrue, that for all I knew he had made it up as he went along; that no tons of rust are scraped off the Menai Bridge, and that the rival tradesmen and Mr. Whiteley were creatures of the poet's brain. Instantly I conceived consuming respect for the man who was so circumstantial, so monotonous, so entirely purposeless a liar. With him it must have been a case of art for art's sake. The joke sustained so gravely through a respected lifetime was of that order of joke which is shared with omniscience. But what struck me more cogently upon reflection was the fact that these immeasurable trivialities, which had struck me as utterly vulgar and arid when I thought they were true, immediately became picturesque and almost brilliant when I thought they were inventions of the human fancy. And here, as it seems to me, I laid my finger upon a fundamental quality of the cultivated class which prevents it, and will, perhaps, always prevent it from seeing with the eyes of popular imagination. The merely educated can scarcely ever be brought to believe that this world is itself an interesting place. When they look at a work of art, good or bad, they expect to be interested, but when they look at a newspaper advertisement or a group in the street, they do not, properly and literally speaking, expect to be interested. But to common and simple people this world is a work of art, though it is, like many great works of art, anonymous. They look to life for interest with the same kind of cheerful and uneradicable assurance with which we look for interest at a comedy for which we have paid money at the door. To the eyes of the ultimate school of contemporary fastidiousness, the universe is indeed an ill-drawn and over-coloured picture, the scrawlings in circles of a baby upon the slate of night; its starry skies are a vulgar pattern which they would not have for a wallpaper, its flowers and fruits have a cockney brilliancy, like the holiday hat of a flower-girl. Hence, degraded by art to its own level, they have lost altogether that primitive and typical taste of man—the taste for news. By this essential taste for news, I mean the pleasure in hearing the mere fact that a man has died at the age of 110 in South Wales, or that the horses ran away at a funeral in San Francisco. Large masses of the early faiths and politics of the world, numbers of the miracles and heroic anecdotes, are based primarily upon this love of something that has just happened, this divine institution of gossip. When Christianity was named the good news, it spread rapidly, not only because it was good, but also because it was news. So it is that if any of us have ever spoken to a navvy in a train about the daily paper, we have generally found the navvy interested, not in those struggles of Parliaments and trades unions which sometimes are, and are always supposed to be, for his benefit; but in the fact that an unusually large whale has been washed up on the coast of Orkney, or that some leading millionaire like Mr. Harmsworth is reported to break a hundred pipes a year. The educated classes, cloyed and demoralized with the mere indulgence of art and mood, can no longer understand the idle and splendid disinterestedness of the reader of *Pearson's Weekly*. He still keeps something of that feeling which should be the birthright of men—the feeling that this planet is like a new house into which we have just moved our baggage. Any detail of it has a value, and, with a truly sportsmanlike instinct, the average man takes most pleasure in the details which are most complicated, irrelevant, and at once difficult and useless to discover. Those parts of the newspaper which announce the giant gooseberry and the raining frogs are really the modern representatives of the popular tendency which produced the hydra and the werewolf and the dog-headed men. Folk in the Middle Ages were not interested in a dragon or a glimpse of the devil because they thought that it was a beautiful prose idyll, but because they thought that it had really just been seen. It was not like so much artistic literature, a refuge indicating the dulness of the world : it was an incident pointedly illustrating the fecund poetry of the world.

That much can be said, and is said, against the literature of information, I do not for a moment deny. It is shapeless, it is trivial, it may give an unreal air of knowledge, it unquestionably lies along with the rest of popular literature under the general indictment that it may spoil the chance of better work, certainly by wasting time, possibly by ruining taste. But these obvious objections are the objections which we hear so persistently from everyone that one cannot help wondering where the papers in question procure their myriads of readers. The natural necessity and natural good underlying such crude institutions is far less often a subject of speculation; yet the healthy hungers which lie at the back of the habits of modern democracy are surely worthy of the same sympathetic study that we give to the dogmas of the fanatics long dethroned and the intrigues of commonwealths long obliterated from the earth. And this is the base and consideration which I have to offer: that perhaps the taste for shreds and patches of journalistic science and history is not, as is continually asserted, the vulgar and senile curiosity of a people that has grown old, but simply the babyish and indiscriminate curiosity of a people still young and entering history for the first time. In other words, I suggest that they only tell each other in magazines the same kind of stories of commonplace portents and conventional eccentricities which, in any case, they would tell each other in taverns. Science itself is only the exaggeration and specialization of this thirst for useless fact, which is the mark of the youth of man. But science has become strangely separated from the mere news and scandal of flowers and birds; men have ceased to see that a pterodactyl was as fresh and natural as a flower, that a flower is as monstrous as a pterodactyl. The rebuilding of this bridge between science and human nature is one of the greatest needs of mankind. We have all to show that before we go on to any visions or creations we can be contented with a planet of miracles.

A DEFENCE OF HERALDRY

THE modern view of heraldry is pretty accurately represented by the words of the famous barrister who, after cross-examining for some time a venerable dignitary of Heralds' College, summed up his results in the remark that 'the silly old man didn't even understand his own silly old trade.'

Heraldry properly so called was, of course, a wholly limited and aristocratic thing, but the remark needs a kind of qualification not commonly realized. In a sense there was a plebeian heraldry, since every shop was, like every castle, distinguished not by a name, but a sign. The whole system dates from a time when picture-writing still really ruled the world. In those days few could read or write; they signed their names with a pictorial symbol, a cross—and a cross is a great improvement on most men's names.

Now, there is something to be said for the peculiar influence of pictorial symbols on men's minds. All letters, we learn, were originally pictorial and heraldic:

thus the letter A is the portrait of an ox, but the portrait is now reproduced in so impressionist a manner that but little of the rural atmosphere can be absorbed by contemplating it. But as long as some pictorial and poetic quality remains in the symbol, the constant use of it must do something for the æsthetic education of those employing it. Public-houses are now almost the only shops that use the ancient signs, and the mysterious attraction which they exercise may be (by the optimistic) explained in this manner. There are taverns with names so dream-like and exquisite that even Sir Wilfrid Lawson might waver on the threshold for a moment, suffering the poet to struggle with the moralist. So it was with the heraldic images. It is impossible to believe that the red lion of Scotland acted upon those employing it merely as a naked convenience like a number or a letter; it is impossible to believe that the Kings of Scotland would have cheerfully accepted the substitute of a pig or a frog. There are, as we say, certain real advantages in pictorial symbols, and one of them is that everything that is pictorial suggests, without naming or defining. There is a road from the eye to the heart that does not go through the intellect. Men do not quarrel about the meaning of sunsets; they never dispute that the hawthorn says the best and wittiest thing about the spring.

Thus in the old aristocratic days there existed this vast pictorial symbolism of all the colours and degrees of aristocracy. When the great trumpet of equality was blown, almost immediately afterwards was made one of the greatest blunders in the history of mankind. For all this pride and vivacity, all these towering symbols and flamboyant colours, should have been extended to mankind. The tobacconist should have had a crest, and the cheese-monger a war-cry. The grocer who sold margarine as butter should have felt that there was a stain on the escutcheon of the Higginses. Instead of doing this, the democrats made the appalling mistake—a mistake at the root of the whole modern malady—of decreasing the human magnificence of the past instead of increasing it. They did not say, as they should have done, to the common citizen, 'You are as good as the Duke of Norfolk,' but used that meaner democratic formula, 'The Duke of Norfolk is no better than you are.'

For it cannot be denied that the world lost something finally and most unfortunately about the beginning of the nineteenth century. In former times the mass of the people was conceived as mean and commonplace, but only as comparatively mean and commonplace; they were dwarfed and eclipsed by certain high stations and splendid callings. But with the Victorian era came a principle which conceived men not as comparatively, but as positively, mean and commonplace. A man of any station was represented as being by nature a dingy and trivial person—a person born, as it were, in a black hat. It began to be thought that it was ridiculous for a man to wear beautiful garments, instead of it being—as, of course, it is—ridiculous for him to deliberately wear ugly ones. It was considered affected for a man to speak bold and heroic words, whereas, of course, it is emotional speech which is natural, and ordinary civil speech which is affected. The whole relations of beauty and ugliness, of dignity and ignominy were turned upside down. Beauty became an extravagance, as if top-hats and umbrellas were not the real extravagance—a landscape from the land of the goblins. Dignity became a form of foolery and shamelessness, as if the very essence of a fool were not a lack of dignity. And the consequence is that it is practically most difficult to propose any decoration or public dignity for modern men without making them laugh. They laugh at the idea of carrying crests and coats-of-arms instead of laughing at their own boots and neckties. We are forbidden to say that tradesmen should have a poetry of their own, although there is nothing so poetical as trade. A grocer should have a coat-of-arms worthy of his strange merchandise gathered from distant and fantastic lands; a postman should have a coat-of-arms capable of expressing the strange honour and responsibility of the man who carries men's souls in a bag; the chemist should have a coat-of-arms symbolizing something of the mysteries of the house of healing, the cavern of a merciful witchcraft.

There were in the French Revolution a class of people at whom everybody laughed, and at whom it was probably difficult, as a practical matter, to refrain from laughing. They attempted to erect, by means of huge wooden statues and brand-new festivals, the most extraordinary new religions. They adored the Goddess of Reason, who would appear, even when the fullest allowance has been made for their many virtues, to be the deity who had least smiled upon them. But these capering maniacs, disowned alike by the old world and the new, were men who had seen a great truth unknown alike to the new world and the old. They had seen the thing that was hidden from the wise and understanding, from the whole modern democratic civilization down to the present time. They realized that democracy must have a heraldry, that it must have a proud and high-coloured pageantry, if it is to keep always before its own mind its own sublime mission. Unfortunately for this ideal, the world has in this matter followed English democracy rather than French; and those who look back to the nineteenth century will assuredly look back to it as we look back to the reign of the Puritans, as the time of black coats and black tempers. From the strange life the men of that time led, they might be assisting at the funeral of liberty instead of at its christening. The moment we really believe in democracy, it will begin to blossom, as aristocracy blossomed, into symbolic colours and shapes. We shall never make anything of democracy until we make fools of ourselves. For if a man really cannot make a fool of himself, we may be quite certain that the effort is superfluous.

A DEFENCE OF UGLY THINGS

THERE are some people who state that the exterior, sex, or physique of another person is indifferent to them, that they care only for the communion of mind with mind; but these people need not detain us. There are some statements that no one ever thinks of believing, however often they are made.

But while nothing in this world would persuade us that a great friend of Mr. Forbes Robertson, let us say, would experience no surprise or discomfort at seeing him enter the room in the bodily form of Mr. Chaplin, there is a confusion constantly made between being attracted by exterior, which is natural and universal, and being attracted by what is called physical beauty, which is not entirely natural and not in the least universal. Or rather, to speak more strictly, the conception of physical beauty has been narrowed to mean a certain kind of physical beauty which no more exhausts the possibilities of external attractiveness than the respectability of a Clapham builder exhausts the possibilities of moral attractiveness.

The tyrants and deceivers of mankind in this matter have been the Greeks. All their splendid work for civilization ought not to have wholly blinded us to the fact of their great and terrible sin against the variety of life. It is a remarkable fact that while the Jews have long ago been rebelled against and accused of blighting the world with a stringent and one-sided ethical standard, nobody has noticed that the Greeks have committed us to an infinitely more horrible asceticism—an asceticism of the fancy, a worship of one æsthetic type alone. Jewish severity had at least common-sense as its basis; it recognised that men lived in a world of fact, and that if a man married within the degrees of blood certain consequences might follow. But they did not starve their instinct for contrasts and combinations; their prophets gave two wings to the ox and any number of eyes to the cherubim with all the riotous ingenuity of Lewis Carroll. But the Greeks carried their police regulation into elfland; they vetoed not the actual adulteries of the earth but the wild weddings of ideas, and forbade the banns of thought.

It is extraordinary to watch the gradual

emasculation of the monsters of Greek myth under the pestilent influence of the Apollo Belvedere. The chimæra was a creature of whom any healthy-minded people would have been proud; but when we see it in Greek pictures we feel inclined to tie a ribbon round its neck and give it a saucer of milk. Who ever feels that the giants in Greek art and poetry were really big—big as some folk-lore giants have been? In some Scandinavian story a hero walks for miles along a mountain ridge, which eventually turns out to be the bridge of the giant's nose. That is what we should call, with a calm conscience, a large giant. But this earthquake fancy terrified the Greeks, and their terror has terrified all mankind out of their natural love of size, vitality, variety, energy, ugliness. Nature intended every human face, so long as it was forcible, individual, and expressive, to be regarded as distinct from all others, as a poplar is distinct from an oak, and an apple-tree from a willow. But what the Dutch gardeners did for trees the Greeks did for the human form; they lopped away its living and sprawling features to give it a certain academic shape; they hacked off noses and pared down chins with a ghastly horticultural calm. And they have really succeeded so far as to make us call some of the most powerful and endearing faces ugly, and some of the most silly and repulsive faces beautiful. This disgraceful *via media*, this pitiful sense of dignity, has bitten far deeper into the soul of modern civilization than the external and practical Puritanism of Israel. The Jew at the worst told a man to dance in fetters; the Greek put an exquisite vase upon his head and told him not to move.

Scripture says that one star differeth from another in glory, and the same conception applies to noses. To insist that one type of face is ugly because it differs from that of the Venus of Milo is to look at it entirely in a misleading light. It is strange that we should resent people differing from ourselves; we should resent much more violently their resembling ourselves. This principle has made a sufficient hash of literary criticism, in which it is always the custom to complain of the lack of sound logic in a fairy tale, and the entire absence of true oratorical power in a three-act farce. But to call another man's face ugly because it powerfully expresses another man's soul is like complaining that a cabbage has not two legs. If we did so, the only course for the cabbage would be to point out with severity, but with some show of truth, that we were not a beautiful green all over.

But this frigid theory of the beautiful has not succeeded in conquering the art of the world, except in name. In some quarters, indeed, it has never held sway. A glance at Chinese dragons or Japanese gods will show how independent are Orientals of the conventional idea of facial and bodily regularity, and how keen and fiery is their enjoyment of real beauty, of goggle eyes, of sprawling claws, of gaping mouths and writhing coils. In the Middle Ages men broke away from the Greek standard of beauty, and lifted up in adoration to heaven great towers, which seemed alive with dancing apes and devils. In the full summer of technical artistic perfection the revolt was carried to its real consummation in the study of the faces of men. Rembrandt declared the sane and manly gospel that a man was dignified, not when he was like a Greek god, but when he had a strong, square nose like a cudgel, a boldly-blocked head like a helmet, and a jaw like a steel trap.

This branch of art is commonly dismissed as the grotesque. We have never been able to understand why it should be humiliating to be laughable, since it is giving an elevated artistic pleasure to others. If a gentleman who saw us in the street were suddenly to burst into tears at the mere thought of our existence, it might be considered disquieting and uncomplimentary; but laughter is not uncomplimentary. In truth, however, the phrase 'grotesque' is a misleading description of ugliness in art. It does not follow that either the Chinese dragons or the Gothic gargoyles or the goblinish old women of Rembrandt were in the least intended to be comic. Their extravagance was not the extravagance of satire, but simply the extravagance of vitality; and here lies the whole key of the place of ugliness in æsthetics. We like to see a crag jut out in shameless decision from the cliff, we like to see the red pines stand up hardily upon a high cliff, we like to see a chasm cloven from end to end of a mountain. With equally noble enthusiasm we like to see a nose jut out decisively, we like to see the red hair of a friend stand up hardily in bristles upon his head, we like to see his mouth broad and clean cut like the mountain crevasse. At least some of us like all this; it is not a question of humour. We do not burst with amusement at the first sight of the pines or the chasm; but we like them because they are expressive of the dramatic stillness of Nature, her bold experiments, her definite departures, her fearlessness and savage pride in her children. The moment we have snapped the spell of conventional beauty, there are a million beautiful faces waiting for us everywhere, just as there are a million beautiful spirits.

A DEFENCE OF FARCE

I HAVE never been able to understand why certain forms of art should be marked off as something debased and trivial. A comedy is spoken of as 'degenerating into farce'; it would be fair criticism to speak of it 'changing into farce'; but as for degenerating into farce, we might equally reasonably speak of it as degenerating into tragedy. Again, a story is spoken of as 'melodramatic,' and the phrase, queerly enough, is not meant as a compliment. To speak of something as 'pantomimic' or 'sensational' is innocently supposed to be biting, Heaven knows why, for all works of art are sensations, and a good pantomime (now extinct) is one of the pleasantest sensations of all. 'This stuff is fit for a detective story,' is often said, as who should say, 'This stuff is fit for an epic.'

Whatever may be the rights and wrongs of this mode of classification, there can be no doubt about one most practical and disastrous effect of it. These lighter or wilder forms of art, having no standard set up for them, no gust of generous artistic pride to lift them up, do actually tend to become as bad as they are supposed to be. Neglected children of the great mother, they grow up in darkness, dirty and unlettered, and when they are right they are right almost by accident, because of the blood in their veins. The common detective story of mystery and murder seems to the intelligent reader to be little except a strange glimpse of a planet peopled by congenital idiots, who cannot find the end of their own noses or the character of their own wives. The common pantomime seems like some horrible satiric picture of a world without cause or effect, a mass of 'jarring atoms,' a prolonged mental torture of irrelevancy. The ordinary farce seems a world of almost piteous vulgarity, where a half-witted and stunted creature is afraid when his wife comes home, and amused when she sits down on the doorstep. All this is, in a sense, true, but it is the fault of nothing in heaven or earth except the attitude and the phrases quoted at the beginning of this article. We have no doubt in the world that, if the other forms of art had been equally despised, they would have been equally despicable. If people had spoken of 'sonnets' with the same accent with which they speak of 'music-hall songs,' a sonnet would have been a thing so fearful and wonderful that we almost regret we cannot have a specimen; a rowdy sonnet is a thing to dream about. If people had said that epics were only fit for children and nursemaids, 'Paradise Lost' might have been an average pantomime: it might have been called 'Harlequin Satan, or How Adam 'Ad 'em.' For who would trouble to bring to perfection a work in which even perfection is grotesque? Why should Shakespeare write 'Othello' if even his triumph consisted in the eulogy, 'Mr. Shakespeare is fit for something better than writing tragedies'?

The case of farce, and its wilder embodiment in harlequinade, is especially important. That these high and legitimate forms of art, glorified by Aristophanes and Molière, have sunk into such contempt may be due to many causes: I myself have little doubt that it is due to the astonishing and ludicrous lack of belief in hope and hilarity which marks modern æsthetics, to such an extent that it has spread even to the revolutionists (once the hopeful section of men), so that even those who ask us to fling the stars into the sea are not quite sure that they will be any better there than they were before. Every form of literary art must be a symbol of some phase of the human spirit; but whereas the phase is, in human life, sufficiently convincing in itself, in art it must have a certain pungency and neatness of form, to compensate for its lack of reality. Thus any set of young people round a tea-table may have all the comedy emotions of 'Much Ado about Nothing' or 'Northanger Abbey,' but if their actual conversation were reported, it would possibly not be a worthy addition to literature. An old man sitting by his fire may have all the desolate grandeur of Lear or Père Goriot, but if he comes into literature he must do something besides sit by the fire. The artistic justification, then, of farce and pantomime must consist in the emotions of life which correspond to them. And these emotions are to an incredible extent crushed out by the modern insistence on the painful side of life only. Pain, it is said, is the dominant element of life; but this is true only in a very special sense. If pain were for one single instant literally the dominant element in life, every man would be found hanging dead from his own bed-post by the morning. Pain, as the black and catastrophic thing, attracts the youthful artist, just as the schoolboy draws devils and skeletons and men hanging. But joy is a far more elusive and elvish matter, since it is our reason for existing, and a very feminine reason; it mingles with every breath we draw and every cup of tea we drink. The literature of joy is infinitely more difficult, more rare and more triumphant than the black and white literature of pain. And of all the varied forms of the literature of joy, the form most truly worthy of moral reverence and artistic ambition is the form called 'farce'—or its wilder shape in pantomime.

To the quietest human being, seated in the quietest house, there will sometimes come a sudden and unmeaning hunger for the possibilities or impossibilities of things; he will abruptly wonder whether the teapot may not suddenly begin to pour out honey or sea-water, the clock to point to all hours of the day at once, the candle to burn green or crimson, the door to open upon a lake or a potato-field instead of a London street. Upon anyone who feels this nameless anarchism there rests for the time being the abiding spirit of pantomime. Of the clown who cuts the policeman in two it may be said (with no darker meaning) that he realizes one of our visions. And it may be noted here that this internal quality in pantomime is perfectly symbolized and preserved by that commonplace or cockney landscape and architecture which characterizes pantomime and farce. If the whole affair happened in some alien atmosphere, if a pear-tree began to grow apples or a river to run with wine in some strange fairyland, the effect would be quite different. The streets and shops and door-knockers of the harlequinade, which to the vulgar æsthete make it seem commonplace, are in truth the very essence of the æsthetic departure. It must be an actual modern door which opens and shuts, constantly disclosing different interiors; it must be a real baker whose loaves fly up into the air without his touching them, or else the whole internal excitement of this elvish invasion of civilization, this abrupt entrance of Puck into Pimlico, is lost. Some day, perhaps, when the present narrow phase of æsthetics has ceased to monopolize the name, the glory of a farcical art may become fashionable. Long after men have ceased to drape their houses in green and gray and to adorn them with Japanese vases, an æsthete may build a house on pantomime principles, in which all the doors shall have their bells and knockers on the inside, all the staircases be constructed to vanish on the pressing of a button, and all the dinners (humorous dinners in themselves) come up cooked through a trapdoor. We are very sure, at least, that it is as reasonable to regulate one's life and lodgings by this kind of art as by any other.

The whole of this view of farce and pantomime may seem insane to us; but we fear that it is we who are insane. Nothing in this strange age of transition is so depressing as its merriment. All the most brilliant men of the day when they set about the writing of comic literature do it under one destructive fallacy and disadvantage: the notion that comic literature is in some sort of way superficial. They give us little knick-knacks of the brittleness of which they positively boast, although two thousand years have beaten as vainly upon the follies of the 'Frogs' as on the wisdom of the 'Republic.' It is all a mean shame of joy. When we come out from a performance of the 'Midsummer Night's Dream' we feel as near to the stars as when we come out from 'King Lear.' For the joy of these works is older than sorrow, their extravagance is saner than wisdom, their love is stronger than death.

The old masters of a healthy madness, Aristophanes or Rabelais or Shakespeare, doubtless had many brushes with the precisians or ascetics of their day, but we cannot but feel that for honest severity and consistent self-maceration they would always have had respect. But what abysses of scorn, inconceivable to any modern, would they have reserved for an æsthetic type and movement which violated morality and did not even find pleasure, which outraged sanity and could not attain to exuberance, which contented itself with the fool's cap without the bells!

A DEFENCE OF HUMILITY

THE act of defending any of the cardinal virtues has to-day all the exhilaration of a vice. Moral truisms have been so much disputed that they have begun to sparkle like so many brilliant paradoxes. And especially (in this age of egoistic idealism) there is about one who defends humility something inexpressibly rakish.

It is no part of my intention to defend humility on practical grounds. Practical grounds are uninteresting, and, moreover, on practical grounds the case for humility is overwhelming. We all know that the 'divine glory of the ego' is socially a great nuisance; we all do actually value our friends for modesty, freshness, and simplicity of heart. Whatever may be the reason, we all do warmly respect humility —in other people.

But the matter must go deeper than this. If the grounds of humility are found only in social convenience, they may be quite trivial and temporary. The egoists may be the martyrs of a nobler dispensation, agonizing for a more arduous ideal.

To judge from the comparative lack of ease in their social manner, this seems a reasonable suggestion.

There is one thing that must be seen at the outset of the study of humility from an intrinsic and eternal point of view. The new philosophy of self-esteem and self-assertion declares that humility is a vice. If it be so, it is quite clear that it is one of those vices which are an integral part of original sin. It follows with the precision of clockwork every one of the great joys of life. No one, for example, was ever in love without indulging in a positive debauch of humility. All full-blooded and natural people, such as schoolboys, enjoy humility the moment they attain hero-worship. Humility, again, is said both by its upholders and opponents to be the peculiar growth of Christianity. The real and obvious reason of this is often missed. The pagans insisted upon self-assertion because it was the essence of their creed that the gods, though strong and just, were mystic, capricious, and even indifferent. But the essence of Christianity was in a literal sense the New Testament —a covenant with God which opened to men a clear deliverance. They thought themselves secure; they claimed palaces of pearl and silver under the oath and seal of the Omnipotent; they believed themselves rich with an irrevocable benediction which set them above the stars; and immediately they discovered humility. It was only another example of the same immutable paradox. It is always the secure who are humble.

This particular instance survives in the evangelical revivalists of the street. They are irritating enough, but no one who has really studied them can deny that the irritation is occasioned by these two things, an irritating hilarity and an irritating humility. This combination of joy and self-prostration is a great deal too universal to be ignored. If humility has been discredited as a virtue at the present day, it is not wholly irrelevant to remark that this discredit has arisen at the same time as a great collapse of joy in current literature and philosophy. Men have revived the splendour of Greek self-assertion at the same time that they have revived the bitterness of Greek pessimism. A literature has arisen which commands us all to arrogate to ourselves the liberty of self-sufficing deities at the same time that it exhibits us to ourselves as dingy maniacs who ought to be chained up like dogs. It is certainly a curious state of things altogether. When we are genuinely happy, we think we are unworthy of happiness. But when we are demanding a divine emancipation we seem to be perfectly certain that we are unworthy of anything.

The only explanation of the matter must be found in the conviction that humility has infinitely deeper roots than any modern men suppose; that it is a metaphysical and, one might almost say, a mathematical virtue. Probably this can best be tested by a study of those who frankly disregard humility and assert the supreme duty of perfecting and expressing one's self. These people tend, by a perfectly natural process, to bring their own great human gifts of culture, intellect, or moral power to a great perfection, successively shutting out everything that they feel to be lower than themselves. Now shutting out things is all very well, but it has one simple corollary—that from everything that we shut out we are ourselves shut out. When we shut our door on the wind, it would be equally true to say that the wind shuts its door on us. Whatever virtues a triumphant egoism really leads to, no one can reasonably pretend that it leads to knowledge. Turning a beggar from the door may be right enough, but pretending to know all the stories the beggar might have narrated is pure nonsense; and this is practically the claim of the egoism which thinks that self-assertion can obtain knowledge. A beetle may or may not be inferior to a man — the matter awaits demonstration; but if he were inferior by ten thousand fathoms, the fact remains that there is probably a beetle view of things of which a man is entirely ignorant. If he wishes to conceive that point of view, he will scarcely reach it by persistently revelling in the fact that he is not a beetle. The most brilliant exponent of the egoistic school, Nietszche, with deadly and honourable logic, admitted that the philosophy of self-satisfaction led to looking down upon the weak, the cowardly, and the ignorant. Looking down on things may be a delightful experience, only there is nothing, from a mountain to a cabbage, that is really *seen* when it is seen from a balloon. The philosopher of the ego sees everything, no doubt, from a high and rarified heaven; only he sees everything foreshortened or deformed.

Now if we imagine that a man wished truly, as far as possible, to see everything as it was, he would certainly proceed on a different principle. He would seek to divest himself for a time of those personal peculiarities which tend to divide him from the thing he studies. It is as difficult, for example, for a man to examine a fish without developing a certain vanity in possessing a pair of legs, as if they were the latest article of personal adornment. But if a fish is to be approximately understood, this physiological dandyism must be overcome. The earnest student of fish morality will, spiritually speaking, chop off his legs. And similarly the student of birds will eliminate his arms; the frog-lover will with one stroke of the imagination remove all his teeth, and the spirit wishing to enter into all the hopes and fears of jelly-fish will simplify his personal appearance to a really alarming extent. It would appear, therefore, that this great body of ours and all its natural instincts, of which we are proud, and justly proud, is rather an encumbrance at the moment when we attempt to appreciate things as they should be appreciated. We do actually go through a process of mental asceticism, a castration of the entire being, when we wish to feel the abounding good in all things. It is good for us at certain times that ourselves should be like a mere window—as clear, as luminous, and as invisible.

In a very entertaining work, over which we have roared in childhood, it is stated that a point has no parts and no magnitude. Humility is the luxurious art of reducing ourselves to a point, not to a small thing or a large one, but to a thing with no size at all, so that to it all the cosmic things are what they really are—of immeasurable stature. That the trees are high and the grasses short is a mere accident of our own foot-rules and our own stature. But to the spirit which has stripped off for a moment its own idle temporal standards the grass is an everlasting forest, with dragons for denizens; the stones of the road are as incredible mountains piled one upon the other; the dandelions are like gigantic bonfires illuminating the lands around; and the heath-bells on their stalks are like planets hung in heaven each higher than the other. Between one stake of a paling and another there are new and terrible landscapes; here a desert, with nothing but one mis-shapen rock; here a miraculous forest, of which all the trees flower above the head with the hues of sunset; here, again, a sea full of monsters that Dante would not have dared to dream. These are the visions of him who, like the child in the fairy tales, is not afraid to become small. Meanwhile, the sage whose faith is in magnitude and ambition is, like a giant, becoming larger and larger, which only means that the stars are becoming smaller and smaller. World after world falls from him into insignificance; the whole passionate and intricate life of common things becomes as lost to him as is the life of the infusoria to a man without a microscope. He rises always through desolate eternities. He may find new systems, and forget them; he may discover fresh universes, and learn to despise them. But the towering and tropical vision of things as they really are—the gigantic daisies, the heaven-consuming dandelions, the great Odyssey of strange-coloured oceans and strange-shaped trees, of dust like the wreck of temples, and thistledown like the ruin of stars—all this colossal vision shall perish with the last of the humble.

A DEFENCE OF SLANG

THE aristocrats of the nineteenth century have destroyed entirely their one solitary utility. It is their business to be flaunting and arrogant; but they flaunt unobtrusively, and their attempts at arrogance are depressing. Their chief duty hitherto has been the development of variety, vivacity, and fulness of life; oligarchy was the world's first experiment in liberty. But now they have adopted the opposite ideal of 'good form,' which may be defined as Puritanism without religion. Good form has sent them all into black like the stroke of a funeral bell. They engage, like Mr. Gilbert's curates, in a war of mildness, a positive competition of obscurity. In old times the lords of the earth sought above all things to be distinguished from each other; with that object they erected outrageous images on their helmets and painted preposterous colours on their shields. They wished to make it entirely clear that a Norfolk was as different, say, from an Argyll as a white lion from a black pig. But to-day their ideal is precisely the opposite one, and if a Norfolk and an Argyll were dressed so much alike that they were mistaken for each other they would both go home dancing with joy.

The consequences of this are inevitable. The aristocracy must lose their function of standing to the world for the idea of variety, experiment, and colour, and we must find these things in some other class. To ask whether we shall find them in the middle class would be to jest upon sacred matters. The only conclusion, therefore, is that it is to certain sections of the lower class, chiefly, for example, to omnibus-conductors, with their rich and rococo mode of thought, that we must look for guidance towards liberty and light.

The one stream of poetry which is continually flowing is slang. Every day a nameless poet weaves some fairy tracery of popular language. It may be said that the fashionable world talks slang as much as the democratic; this is true, and it strongly supports the view under consideration. Nothing is more startling than the contrast between the heavy, formal, lifeless slang of the man-about-town and the light, living, and flexible slang of the coster. The talk of the upper strata of the educated classes is about the most shapeless, aimless, and hopeless literary product that the world has ever seen. Clearly in this, again, the upper classes have degenerated. We have ample evidence that the old leaders of feudal war could speak on occasion with a certain natural symbolism and eloquence that they had not gained from books. When Cyrano de Bergerac, in Rostand's play, throws doubts on the reality of Christian's dulness and lack of culture, the latter replies :

> 'Bah! on trouve des mots quand on monte à l'assaut;
> Oui, j'ai un certain esprit facile et militaire ;'

and these two lines sum up a truth about the old oligarchs. They could not write three legible letters, but they could sometimes speak literature. Douglas, when he hurled the heart of Bruce in front of him in his last battle, cried out, 'Pass first, great heart, as thou wert ever wont.' A Spanish nobleman, when commanded by the King to receive a high-placed and notorious traitor, said : 'I will receive him in all obedience, and burn down my house afterwards.' This is literature without culture ; it is the speech of men convinced that they have to assert proudly the poetry of life.

Anyone, however, who should seek for such pearls in the conversation of a young man of modern Belgravia would have much sorrow in his life. It is not only impossible for aristocrats to assert proudly the poetry of life ; it is more impossible for them than for anyone else. It is positively considered vulgar for a nobleman to boast of his ancient name, which is, when one comes to think of it, the only rational object of his existence. If a man in the street proclaimed, with rude feudal rhetoric, that he was the Earl of Doncaster, he would be arrested as a lunatic ; but if it were discovered that he really was the Earl of Doncaster, he would simply be cut as a cad. No poetical prose must be expected from Earls as a class. The fashionable slang is hardly even a language ; it is like the formless cries of animals, dimly indicating certain broad, well-understood states of mind. 'Bored,' 'cut up,' 'jolly,' 'rotten,' and so on, are like the words of some tribe of savages whose vocabulary has only twenty of them. If a man of fashion wished to protest against some solecism in another man of fashion, his utterance would be a mere string of set phrases, as lifeless as a string of dead fish. But an omnibus conductor (being filled with the Muse) would burst out into a solid literary effort : 'You're a gen'leman, aren't yer . . . yer boots is a lot brighter than yer 'ed . . . there's precious little of yer, and that's clothes . . . that's right, put yer cigar in yer mouth 'cos I can't see yer be'ind it . . . take it out again, do yer! you're young for smokin', but I've sent for yer mother. . . . Goin'? oh, don't run away: I won't 'arm yer. I've got a good 'art, I 'ave. . . . "Down with croolty to animals," I say,' and so on. It is evident that this mode of speech is not only literary, but literary in a very ornate and almost artificial sense. Keats never put into a sonnet so many remote metaphors as a coster puts into a curse; his speech is one long allegory, like Spenser's 'Faerie Queen.'

I do not imagine that it is necessary to demonstrate that this poetic allusiveness is the characteristic of true slang. Such an expression as 'Keep your hair on' is positively Meredithian in its perverse and mysterious manner of expressing an idea. The Americans have a well-known expression about 'swelled-head' as a description of self-approval, and the other day I heard a remarkable fantasia upon this air. An American said that after the Chinese War the Japanese wanted 'to put on their hats with a shoe-horn.' This is a monument of the true nature of slang, which consists in getting further and further away from the original conception, in treating it more and more as an assumption. It is rather like the literary doctrine of the Symbolists.

The real reason of this great development of eloquence among the lower orders again brings us back to the case of the aristocracy in earlier times. The lower classes live in a state of war, a war of words. Their readiness is the product of the same fiery individualism as the readiness of the old fighting oligarchs. Any cabman has to be ready with his tongue, as any gentleman of the last century had to be ready with his sword. It is unfortunate that the poetry which is developed by this process should be purely a grotesque poetry. But as the higher orders of society have entirely abdicated their right to speak with a heroic eloquence, it is no wonder that the language should develop by itself in the direction of a rowdy eloquence. The essential point is that somebody must be at work adding new symbols and new circumlocutions to a language.

All slang is metaphor, and all metaphor is poetry. If we paused for a moment to examine the cheapest cant phrases that pass our lips every day, we should find that they were as rich and suggestive as so many sonnets. To take a single instance:

we speak of a man in English social relations 'breaking the ice.' If this were expanded into a sonnet, we should have before us a dark and sublime picture of an ocean of everlasting ice, the sombre and baffling mirror of the Northern nature, over which men walked and danced and skated easily, but under which the living waters roared and toiled fathoms below. The world of slang is a kind of topsy-turveydom of poetry, full of blue moons and white elephants, of men losing their heads, and men whose tongues run away with them—a whole chaos of fairy tales.

A DEFENCE OF BABY-WORSHIP

THE two facts which attract almost every normal person to children are, first, that they are very serious, and, secondly, that they are in consequence very happy. They are jolly with the completeness which is possible only in the absence of humour. The most unfathomable schools and sages have never attained to the gravity which dwells in the eyes of a baby of three months old. It is the gravity of astonishment at the universe, and astonishment at the universe is not mysticism, but a transcendent common-sense. The fascination of children lies in this: that with each of them all things are remade, and the universe is put again upon its trial. As we walk the streets and see below us those delightful bulbous heads, three times too big for the body, which mark these human mushrooms, we ought always primarily to remember that within every one of these heads there is a new universe, as new as it was on the seventh day of creation. In each of those orbs there is a new system of stars, new grass, new cities, a new sea.

There is always in the healthy mind an obscure prompting that religion teaches us rather to dig than to climb ; that if we could once understand the common clay of earth we should understand everything. Similarly, we have the sentiment that if we could destroy custom at a blow and see the stars as a child sees them, we should need no other apocalypse. This is the great truth which has always lain at the back of baby-worship, and which will support it to the end. Maturity, with its endless energies and aspirations, may easily be convinced that it will find new things to appreciate ; but it will never be convinced, at bottom, that it has properly appreciated what it has got. We may scale the heavens and find new stars innumerable, but there is still the new star we have not found—that on which we were born.

But the influence of children goes further than its first trifling effort of remaking heaven and earth. It forces us actually to remodel our conduct in accordance with this revolutionary theory of the marvellousness of all things. We do (even when we are perfectly simple or ignorant)—we do actually treat talking in children as marvellous, walking in children as marvellous, common intelligence in children as marvellous. The cynical philosopher fancies he has a victory in this matter—that he can laugh when he shows that the words or antics of the child, so much admired by its worshippers, are common enough. The fact is that this is precisely where baby-worship is so profoundly right. Any words and any antics in a lump of clay are wonderful, the child's words and antics are wonderful, and it is only fair to say that the philosopher's words and antics are equally wonderful.

The truth is that it is our attitude towards children that is right, and our attitude towards grown-up people that is wrong. Our attitude towards our equals in age consists in a servile solemnity, overlying a considerable degree of indifference or disdain. Our attitude towards children consists in a condescending indulgence, overlying an unfathomable respect. We bow to grown people, take off our hats to them, refrain from contradicting them flatly, but we do not appreciate them properly. We make puppets of children, lecture them, pull their hair, and reverence, love, and fear them. When we reverence anything in the mature, it is their virtues or their wisdom, and this is an easy matter. But we reverence the faults and follies of children.

We should probably come considerably nearer to the true conception of things if we treated all grown-up persons, of all titles and types, with precisely that dark affection and dazed respect with which we treat the infantile limitations. A child has a difficulty in achieving the miracle of speech, consequently we find his blunders almost as marvellous as his accuracy. If we only adopted the same attitude towards Premiers and Chancellors of the Exchequer, if we genially encouraged their stammering and delightful attempts at human speech, we should be in a far more wise and tolerant temper. A child has a knack of making experiments in life, generally healthy in motive, but often intolerable in a domestic commonwealth. If we only treated all commercial buccaneers and bumptious tyrants on the same terms, if we gently chided their brutalities as rather quaint mistakes in the conduct of life, if we simply told them that they would 'understand when they were older,' we should probably be adopting the best and most crushing attitude towards the weaknesses of humanity. In our relations to children we prove that the paradox is entirely true, that it is possible to combine an amnesty that verges on contempt with a worship that verges upon terror. We forgive children with the same kind of blasphemous gentleness with which Omar Khayyam forgave the Omnipotent.

The essential rectitude of our view of children lies in the fact that we feel them and their ways to be supernatural while, for some mysterious reason, we do not feel ourselves or our own ways to be supernatural. The very smallness of children makes it possible to regard them as marvels; we seem to be dealing with a new race, only to be seen through a microscope. I doubt if anyone of any tenderness or imagination can see the hand of a child and not be a little frightened of it. It is awful to think of the essential human energy moving so tiny a thing; it is like imagining that human nature could live in the wing of a butterfly or the leaf of a tree. When we look upon lives so human and yet so small, we feel as if we ourselves were enlarged to an embarrassing bigness of stature. We feel the same kind of obligation to these creatures that a deity might feel if he had created something that he could not understand.

But the humorous look of children is perhaps the most endearing of all the bonds that hold the Cosmos together.

Their top-heavy dignity is more touching than any humility; their solemnity gives us more hope for all things than a thousand carnivals of optimism; their large and lustrous eyes seem to hold all the stars in their astonishment; their fascinating absence of nose seems to give to us the most perfect hint of the humour that awaits us in the kingdom of heaven.

A DEFENCE OF DETECTIVE STORIES

IN attempting to reach the genuine psychological reason for the popularity of detective stories, it is necessary to rid ourselves of many mere phrases. It is not true, for example, that the populace prefer bad literature to good, and accept detective stories because they are bad literature. The mere absence of artistic subtlety does not make a book popular. Bradshaw's Railway Guide contains few gleams of psychological comedy, yet it is not read aloud uproariously on winter evenings. If detective stories are read with more exuberance than railway guides, it is certainly because they are more artistic. Many good books have fortunately been popular; many bad books, still more fortunately, have been unpopular. A good detective story would probably be even more popular than a bad one. The trouble in this matter is that many people do not realize that there is such a thing as a good detective story; it is to them like speaking of a good devil. To write a story about a burglary is, in their eyes, a sort of spiritual manner of committing it. To persons of somewhat weak sensibility this is natural enough; it must be confessed that many detective stories are as full of sensational crime as one of Shakespeare's plays.

There is, however, between a good detective story and a bad detective story as much, or, rather more, difference than there is between a good epic and a bad one. Not only is a detective story a perfectly legitimate form of art, but it has certain definite and real advantages as an agent of the public weal.

The first essential value of the detective story lies in this, that it is the earliest and only form of popular literature in which is expressed some sense of the poetry of modern life. Men lived among mighty mountains and eternal forests for ages before they realized that they were poetical; it may reasonably be inferred that some of our descendants may see the chimney-pots as rich a purple as the mountain-peaks, and find the lamp-posts as old and natural as the trees. Of this realization of a great city itself as something wild and obvious the detective story is certainly the 'Iliad. No one can have failed to notice that in these stories the hero or the investigator crosses London with something of the loneliness and liberty of a prince in a tale of elfland, that in the course of that incalculable journey the casual omnibus assumes the primal colours of a fairy ship. The lights of the city begin to glow like innumerable goblin eyes, since they are the guardians of some secret, however crude, which the writer knows and the reader does not. Every twist of the road is like a finger pointing to it; every fantastic skyline of chimney-pots seems wildly and derisively signalling the meaning of the mystery.

This realization of the poetry of London is not a small thing. A city is, properly speaking, more poetic even than a countryside, for while Nature is a chaos of unconscious forces, a city is a chaos of conscious ones. The crest of the flower or the pattern of the lichen may or may not be significant symbols. But there is no stone in the street and no brick in the wall that is not actually a deliberate symbol—a message from some man, as much as if it were a telegram or a post-card. The narrowest street possesses, in every crook and twist of its intention, the soul of the man who built it, perhaps long in his grave. Every brick has as human a hieroglyph as if it were a graven brick of Babylon; every slate on the roof is as educational a document as if it were a slate covered with addition and subtraction sums. Anything which tends, even under the fantastic form of the minutiæ of Sherlock Holmes, to assert this romance of detail in civilization, to emphasize this unfathomably human character in flints and tiles, is a good thing. It is good that the average man should fall into the habit of looking imaginatively at ten men in the street even if it is only on the chance that the eleventh might be a notorious thief. We may dream, perhaps, that it might be possible to have another and higher romance of London, that men's souls have stranger adventures than their bodies, and that it would be harder and more exciting to hunt their virtues than to hunt their crimes. But since our great authors (with the admirable exception of Stevenson) decline to write of that thrilling mood and moment when the eyes of the great city, like the eyes of a cat, begin to flame in the dark, we must give fair credit to the popular literature which, amid a babble of pedantry and preciosity, declines to regard the present as prosaic or the common as commonplace. Popular art in all ages has been interested in contemporary manners and costume; it dressed the groups around the Crucifixion in the garb of Florentine gentlefolk or Flemish burghers. In the last century it was the custom for distinguished actors to present Macbeth in a powdered wig and ruffles. How far we are ourselves in this age from such conviction of the poetry of our own life and manners may easily be conceived by anyone who chooses to imagine a picture of Alfred the Great toasting the cakes dressed in tourist's knickerbockers, or a performance of 'Hamlet' in which the Prince appeared in a frock-coat, with a crape band round his hat. But this instinct of the age to look back, like Lot's wife, could not go on for ever. A rude, popular literature of the romantic possibilities of the modern city was bound to arise. It has arisen in the popular detective stories, as rough and refreshing as the ballads of Robin Hood.

There is, however, another good work that is done by detective stories. While it is the constant tendency of the Old Adam to rebel against so universal and automatic a thing as civilization, to preach departure and rebellion, the romance of police activity keeps in some sense before the mind the fact that civilization itself is the most sensational of departures and the most romantic of rebellions. By dealing with the unsleeping sentinels who guard the outposts of society, it tends to remind us that we live in an armed camp, making war with a chaotic world, and that the criminals, the children of chaos, are nothing but the traitors within our gates. When the detective in a police romance stands alone, and somewhat fatuously fearless amid the knives and fists of a thieves' kitchen, it does certainly serve to make us remember that it is the agent of social justice who is the original and poetic figure, while the burglars and footpads are merely placid old cosmic conservatives, happy in the immemorial respectability of apes and wolves. The romance of the police force is thus the whole romance of man. It is based on the fact that morality is the most dark and daring of conspiracies. It reminds us that the whole noiseless and unnoticeable police management by which we are ruled and protected is only a successful knight-errantry.

A DEFENCE OF PATRIOTISM

THE decay of patriotism in England during the last year or two is a serious and distressing matter. Only in consequence of such a decay could the current lust of territory be confounded with the ancient love of country. We may imagine that if there were no such thing as a pair of lovers left in the world, all the vocabulary of love might without rebuke be transferred to the lowest and most automatic desire. If no type of chivalrous and purifying passion remained, there would be no one left to say that lust bore none of the marks of love, that lust was rapacious and love pitiful, that lust was blind and love vigilant, that lust sated itself and love was insatiable. So it is with the 'love of the city,' that high and ancient intellectual passion which has been written in red blood on the same table with the primal passions of our being. On all sides we hear to-day of the love of our country, and yet anyone who has literally such a love must be bewildered at the talk, like a man hearing all men say that the moon shines by day and the sun by night. The conviction must come to him at last that these men do not realize what the word 'love' means, that they mean by the love of country, not what a mystic might mean by the love of God, but something of what a child might mean by the love of jam. To one who loves his fatherland, for instance, our boasted indifference to the ethics of a national war is mere mysterious gibberism. It is like telling a man that a boy has committed murder, but that he need not mind because it is only his son. Here clearly the word 'love' is used unmeaningly. It is the essence of love to be sensitive, it is a part of its doom; and anyone who objects to the one must certainly get rid of the other. This sensitiveness, rising sometimes to an almost morbid sensitiveness, was the mark of all great lovers like Dante and all great patriots like Chatham. 'My country, right or wrong,' is a thing that no patriot would think of saying except in a desperate case. It is like saying, 'My mother, drunk or sober.' No doubt if a decent man's mother took to drink he would share her troubles to the last; but to talk as if he would be in a state of gay indifference as to whether his mother took to drink or not is certainly not the language of men who know the great mystery.

What we really need for the frustration and overthrow of a deaf and raucous Jingoism is a renascence of the love of the native land. When that comes, all shrill cries will cease suddenly. For the first of all the marks of love is seriousness: love will not accept sham bulletins or the empty victory of words. It will always esteem the most candid counsellor the best. Love is drawn to truth by the unerring magnetism of agony; it gives no pleasure to the lover to see ten doctors dancing with vociferous optimism round a death-bed.

We have to ask, then, Why is it that this recent movement in England, which has honestly appeared to many a renascence of patriotism, seems to us to have none of the marks of patriotism—at least, of patriotism in its highest form? Why has the adoration of our patriots been given wholly to qualities and circumstances good in themselves, but comparatively material and trivial:—trade, physical force, a skirmish at a remote frontier, a squabble in a remote continent? Colonies are things to be proud of, but for a country to be only proud of its extremities is like a man being only proud of his legs. Why is there not a high central intellectual patriotism, a patriotism of the head and heart of the Empire, and not merely of its fists and its boots? A rude Athenian sailor may very likely have thought that the glory of Athens lay in rowing with the right kind of oars, or having a good supply of garlic; but Pericles did not think that this was the glory of Athens. With us, on the other hand, there is no difference at all between the patriotism preached by Mr. Chamberlain and that preached by Mr. Pat Rafferty, who sings 'What do you think of the Irish now?' They are both honest, simple-minded, vulgar eulogies upon trivialities and truisms.

I have, rightly or wrongly, a notion of the chief cause of this pettiness in English patriotism of to-day, and I will attempt to expound it. It may be taken generally that a man loves his own stock and environment, and that he will find something to praise in it; but whether it is the most praiseworthy thing or no will depend upon the man's enlightenment as to the facts. If the son of Thackeray, let us say, were brought up in ignorance of his father's fame and genius, it is not improbable that he would be proud of the fact that his father was over six feet high. It seems to me that we, as a nation, are precisely in the position of this hypothetical child of Thackeray's.

We fall back upon gross and frivolous things for our patriotism, for a simple reason. We are the only people in the world who are not taught in childhood our own literature and our own history.

We are, as a nation, in the truly extraordinary condition of not knowing our own merits. We have played a great and splendid part in the history of universal thought and sentiment; we have been among the foremost in that eternal and bloodless battle in which the blows do not slay, but create. In painting and music we are inferior to many other nations; but in literature, science, philosophy, and political eloquence, if history be taken as a whole, we can hold our own with any. But all this vast heritage of intellectual glory is kept from our schoolboys like a heresy; and they are left to live and die in the dull and infantile type of patriotism which they learnt from a box of tin soldiers. There is no harm in the box of tin soldiers; we do not expect children to be equally delighted with a beautiful box of tin philanthropists. But there is great harm in the fact that the subtler and more civilized honour of England is not presented so as to keep pace with the expanding mind. A French boy is taught the glory of Molière as well as that of Turenne; a German boy is taught his own great national philosophy before he learns the philosophy of antiquity. The result is that, though French patriotism is often crazy and boastful, though German patriotism is often isolated and pedantic, they are neither of them merely dull, common, and brutal, as is so often the strange fate of the nation of Bacon and Locke. It is natural enough, and even righteous enough, under the circumstances. An Englishman must love England for something; consequently, he tends to exalt commerce or prize-fighting, just as a German might tend to exalt music, or a Flamand to exalt painting, because he really believes it is the chief merit of his fatherland. It would not be in the least extraordinary if a claim of eating up provinces and pulling down princes were the chief boast of a Zulu. The extraordinary thing is, that it is the chief boast of a people who have Shakespeare, Newton, Burke, and Darwin to boast of.

The peculiar lack of any generosity or delicacy in the current English nationalism appears to have no other possible origin but in this fact of our unique neglect in education of the study of the national literature. An Englishman could not be silly enough to despise other nations if he once knew how much England had done for them. Great men of letters cannot avoid being humane and universal. The absence of the teaching of English literature in our schools is, when we come to think of it, an almost amazing phenomenon. It is even more amazing when we listen to the arguments urged by head-masters and other educational conservatives against the direct teaching of English. It is said, for example, that a vast amount of English grammar and literature is picked up in the course of learning Latin and Greek. This is perfectly true, but the topsy-turviness of the idea never seems to strike them. It is like saying that a baby picks up the art of walking in the course of learning to hop, or that a Frenchman may successfully be taught German by helping a Prussian to learn Ashanti. Surely the obvious foundation of all education is the language in which that education is conveyed; if a boy has only time to learn one thing, he had better learn that.

We have deliberately neglected this great heritage of high national sentiment. We have made our public schools the strongest walls against a whisper of the honour of England. And we have had our punishment in this strange and perverted fact that, while a unifying vision of patriotism can ennoble bands of brutal savages or dingy burghers, and be the best thing in their lives, we, who are—the world being judge—humane, honest, and serious individually, have a patriotism that is the worst thing in ours. What have we done, and where have we wandered, we that have produced sages who could have spoken with Socrates and poets who could walk with Dante, that we should talk as if we have never done anything more intelligent than found colonies and kick niggers? We are the children of light, and it is we that sit in darkness. If we are judged, it will not be for the merely intellectual transgression of failing to appreciate other nations, but for the supreme spiritual transgression of failing to appreciate ourselves.

THE END

BILLING AND SONS, LTD., PRINTERS, GUILDFORD